GRABBING
AT
WATER

A Mother-Daughter Memoir

JOAN AND MADELEINE LAMBUR

SSE

SIMON SPOTLIGHT ENTERTAINMENT
New York London Toronto Sydney

Certain names and identifying characteristics have been changed.

SSE

SIMON SPOTLIGHT ENTERTAINMENT
An imprint of Simon & Schuster
1230 Avenue of the Americas, New York, New York 10020
Copyright © 2008 by Joan Lambur
All rights reserved, including the right of reproduction in whole or
in part in any form.
SIMON SPOTLIGHT ENTERTAINMENT and related logo are trademarks of
Simon & Schuster, Inc.
Designed by Gabe Levine
Manufactured in the United States of America
First Edition
2 4 6 8 10 9 7 5 3 1
Library of Congress Cataloging-in-Publication Data
Lambur, Joan.
Grabbing at water : a mother-daughter memoir /
by Joan and Madeleine Lambur.—1st ed.
p. cm.
ISBN-13: 978-1-4169-1839-4
ISBN-10: 1-4169-1839-6
1. Mothers and daughters—Biography. 2. Mothers and daughters—Humor.
3. Parent and adult child. I. Lambur, Madeleine. II. Title.
HQ755.86.L36 2008
306.874'3092—dc22
[B]
2007025401

To my mom —*J. L.*

To my mom and dad —*M. L.*

Contents

JOAN'S INTRODUCTION

I was not pretty when I was pregnant. I looked like hell—acne; dull, straight hair; violent, bright purple stretch marks; and a belly so huge that by my third trimester I couldn't fit into a booth at a restaurant. On top of being ugly, I threw up each and every day for nine months.

My first pregnancy, with my son, Ian, was rough, but it was a joyride compared with my second pregnancy, with my daughter, Maddy. From the fifth month she wielded the brute force of a wild toddler. At first I thought her rowdy behavior was cute, and I was secretly proud of the fact that this tyke was quite the little tiger. By the last couple of months of my pregnancy, however, it wasn't so cute, and I found myself spending more and more time wrestling with my unborn little darling. She insisted on jamming her foot under my ribs, for instance, and when I would gently try and shift it, she would kick back with the force of an angry billy goat. I think I was one of the first and only mothers who fought with her unborn child. I sometimes wondered if it would be okay to give her a spanking even before she was born, but then I realized I was hormonally unbalanced for even thinking such a thing.

By the time Maddy was born, I was even bigger than I had been with Ian. When my doctor came to see me the night before I was to have my scheduled C-section (yes, she was just that massive!), he took one look at me and froze. He swore that this baby had gained at least a pound in the few days since I had last seen him.

What's funny is that all through my pregnancy with Maddy, I was absolutely convinced that I was having another boy. I had even compiled a list of great boys' names and was ready to live my life with a house full of men. The kicking, the pushing, the wrestling matches in my womb—all of it had me convinced I was having a burly bruiser.

No one was more shocked than I when my doctor pulled a screaming, dark-haired, enormous baby out of me and announced: "It's a girl!"

I couldn't believe it was true. At Ian's birth there had been no emotional tears because I was so exhausted after thirteen hours of fruitless labor and having been sliced practically from chin to knees (no fancy "bikini" cut for this mother). I was just trying to survive his arrival. Maddy, on the other hand, was a scheduled C-section, so I was fairly alert and together. But when I looked at her for the first time, I cried.

My little girl was absolutely gorgeous. She had a shock of

black hair and a big potbelly with a scream to match. Once I got back to my hospital room (happily with a hit of Demerol), I settled into getting to know her. Her fingers were so tiny, her eyes so wide and determined. I must have stared at her for hours that night. She was perfect.

Her father and I just couldn't come up with a name we both loved. I, for some reason, was stuck on "Madeleine."

"Think of it," I remember saying to him, "Madeleine Lambur. It will look perfect on a book cover."

I wanted the world for her.

He relented immediately and agreed to Madeleine, but only under the condition that I give her my own name as her middle name.

Madeleine Joan Lambur.

Nine months of kicking and fighting inside of me, and there she was all wrapped up and swaddled, looking up at me, just hours old, with my name—a small, symbolic piece of me—following right after her own.

Maddy's Introduction

One of my first memories of my mom is of a game we used to play when I was five. At the time, I didn't see it as a game but more as a challenge of strength. Granted I was only five years old, but my mom had already somehow instilled in me the belief that I could achieve anything I set my mind to.

Every day after kindergarten, she picked me up from school. I always saw her waiting at the bottom of the steps, ready with a smile. We walked toward home, talking about I can't remember what, sometimes holding hands, sometimes not.

Once we got exactly one block from our house, I stopped and looked up at her. She pretended not to notice and kept talking and walking ahead of me, leaving me where I was, all alone, until she got to the end of the block.

At the end of the block, she turned around, faced me,

crouched down, and opened her arms as wide as they could go. That was my signal.

That's when I took a deep breath and started running as fast as my legs would carry me, my shoes slapping the pavement. Run, run, run. The feeling of my hair and my cheeks flapping in the wind was like the feeling a dog probably gets when he sticks his head out a car window—or the feeling an Olympic sprinter gets when she's inches from the finish line. It was completely exhilarating. It was complete freedom. I just let go and ran.

As I got closer, I remember seeing my mother start to smile as she adjusted her feet and readied herself from her crouching position for what was to come next.

Closer and closer I got, and then BAM! I ran straight into her open arms with my full force and knocked her over. That was our game, and I always won.

After I collided into her, she always fell backward onto the sidewalk with her arms wrapped tightly around me, and we both started laughing. Then she rolled over, still holding me, and laughed so hard I thought she would burst.

Looking back now, I know she let me win. I was five years old after all. But she let me believe in my power, and she never let me get hurt.

I still remember that game like it was yesterday—whenever I'm running too fast, or when life feels like too much for me—I remember the feeling of her arms wrapped tightly around me.

CHAPTER 1

SAINT JOAN

Joan

As an Irish Catholic I feel guilty and unsure about pretty much everything in my life. That said, there have been a couple of exceptions—such as how I felt about my two kids and how I was going to raise them. Back in my day, growing up as a Catholic girl, going to Catholic school, hanging out with Catholic friends and relatives, and being at the mercy of Catholic-style discipline, I learned how not to raise my kids.

Our parents were convinced that if they ever, ever threw us kids a compliment, we would get "big heads"—which meant that we would become intolerable, conceited asses that no one (especially God) would want to have anything to do with. Feeling good about yourself was not acceptable, and you better not for one second think you're good-looking—because then you were a real sinner.

As a result I grew up certain that I was ugly enough that people stopped on the street just to look. It really was a bit of a problem but not something I could talk to anyone about because that would be vain, and vanity was a sin. To add insult to injury, I had red hair—which everyone knew meant you had a terrible, uncontrollable temper that had to be treated very aggressively. The nuns especially had real difficulty with the red mane and assumed that anyone sporting one was nothing but trouble. My mom gave me my first self-help book when I was six years old in the early sixties, when the self-help industry was barely off the ground. It was a book for kids called *I Have a Temper*.

This did nothing but aggravate me further and drive me to slam my head against the wall, slam doors, and generally fuel the preconceived notions being thrown my way. It's true that redheads can be pretty hotheaded, but I wasn't going to admit it then. Punishments back in those days were quite something. We were hit with a yardstick—known as just "the stick"—and getting hit on Sundays after Mass was pretty much a sure bet. Out of us four kids, somehow I was the one who managed to find myself in the lineup every week. I swore to myself during those very tragic moments (I was a drama queen even then) that I would never, ever, EVER treat my children that way. Not only would I compliment the hell out of them, but I would never hit them. Well, it was true I didn't (almost never); instead I took punishment to a new level and employed psychological warfare—so much for evolution.

I have always prided myself on being a fair, yet firm and

loving parent. With the exception of a couple of years when the kids were teens and I was absolutely full-out menopausal (or perimenopausal or whatever you want to call it), I think I have been incredibly effective with my kids and in some instances with other people's kids. In spite of my current obsession with self-improvement books, I never really felt I needed help when the kids were younger because I truly believed I was born to parent and that my instincts were right on the money.

Despite the fact that my two delightful offspring have made it a hobby to tell anyone who will listen how completely ridiculous and totally ineffective I was with tots and teens in times of trouble, I still maintain that I was one of the greats at coming up with unbelievably creative punishments that taught invaluable life lessons. As a small example, I believed that if they bit, they should be bitten back. Now, I have since seen the likes of Dr. Phil speak out vehemently against such draconian measures, but I question whether ol' Dr. Phil ever actually got bitten in the face by a little creature with vampire-like fangs, and if he had, what he really would have done.

I'm sure I should have sent Maddy or Ian on a time-out; or asked that they spend time on the naughty mat; or spoken to them in my indoor voice, asked them nicely not to break Mommy's skin again, and to express themselves with words. Whatever! I don't have a clue how any mother can do anything but raise a complete savage with those limitations—it may not be popular, but from where I sat, it was war every day, and I had no intention of losing.

One of my shining moments occurred one day when I

was grocery shopping with my kids—Ian was ten and Maddy was eight—and my best friend's two kids, Lauren and Patrick. They were always a dangerous unit because Lauren, who was also eight, could teach Maddy things that good old Ian, being a sweet, naive male, had never even thought of.

I had recently split up with my husband and was into my second year of fending for myself. At any given time, our basement was backed up knee-deep in sewage, or the pipes had burst, or the kids had pulled the bathroom sink off the wall, causing a flood, or the front lawn was being dug up because of the sewage problem, or the utilities were being cut off because I couldn't pay the bills. Suffice it to say, my life wasn't going so smoothly, but we had love—which, of course, every one of my favorite songs said was enough. Career wise, I had been working for a talent agency. Unfortunately, however, six months into my stint my paychecks began bouncing. Of course, that triggered the bouncing of all the checks I had written that month—further destroying my already pathetic credit rating. Oh well, it really wasn't the end of the world because my boss, along the way, had decided he wanted to give me a makeover. He'd bought me incredibly expensive clothes and paid for a body wave that would make any self-respecting eighties chick green with envy. With my hot, post-divorce body and my new wardrobe and hair, I really couldn't get that down over the state of my life. And on top of it all, I was able to sign on some of my boss's actors (all completely crazy and neurotic but moneymakers nonetheless) and start my own talent agency. After all, I had six months of work experience—how hard could it be? Well, six years, a million cigarettes, ten thousand beers, and thirty pounds later, I was living proof that it wasn't quite as simple as I thought it would be. . . .

But back to the kids. I'm at the store with the four kids who, when together, were total maniacs complete with dirty faces and badass attitudes. When together, we had been thrown out of restaurants several times, and we certainly had our respective communities under the impression the kids were going to grow up to be felons—not that far off as it turned out, at least not for the darling girls.

At the grocery store the boys were running around like banshees. I'm still not clear on what they were trying to accomplish, but I'm sure it had something to do with war and intrigue. The girls, however, were being a lot quieter and were loitering around the candy bins. I warned them to keep their grimy paws out of those things and threatened them within an inch of their lives if they didn't. I ran over to another aisle to get something—probably a large box of Kraft Macaroni & Cheese Dinner. (Yes, I was a very bad mother for not feeding the younguns something organic, but what the hell was I supposed to do when I was so broke?)

I was running around the place like an idiot with my eyes peeled for the four hoodlums when I discovered the girls huddled in the corner of the bulk-bin area with their backs to me. I knew instinctively that some crime had been committed. I decided to creep up behind them so I could startle them and hopefully get the truth out of them without too much torture—because frankly I was kind of tired that day and just wanted to get back home and chill out. Sure enough, they were whispering like thieves and cooking up some kind of scheme. I called their names sharply, and they turned around with their faces absolutely covered in candy and sugar; they looked like they had been dragged through a vat of the stuff. They had it all over their snowsuits, hair, and hands.

In my firmest voice I demanded to know what was going on, and they had the total cheek to look at me with their big eyes and say, "Nothing!" I asked them if they had been stealing candy from the bins, and they looked at me as though they were insulted that I would dare to insinuate such a thing. They were unbelievable! I pointed out that they were covered in the evidence, and they looked terrified and knew they were busted. When they told me that they had only taken one each and that they were really, really sorry, I told them that it was out of my hands and that I had no choice but to turn them into the authorities.

I took them over to the store manager. Luckily, she was as twisted as I was and played right along with me. Even better, she was big and ugly and mean looking. I explained the whole sordid situation to her, while their candy-covered faces stared up at her (they really did look pretty cute), absolutely terrified that they were going to be doing some hard time. She and I discussed at length the prospect of calling the police and having them take the kids into the station for fingerprinting and mug shots. Fantastic! We speculated about whether they would go to prison and concluded that they probably wouldn't because of school and stuff. We also figured they were too young and inexperienced to be able to make license plates or do laundry in jail.

After a lengthy discussion and a couple of fake moves toward the phone, the manager decided she would let them "walk" this time, but God help them if they ever tried anything like that again. Boy, was I proud that they had learned such an important lesson at such a young age, and it was all thanks to me. These girls would never steal again.

I then took the perps and their male counterparts home and made the girls do chores all day long. It worked out really well for me, since I had a ton of laundry that needed folding, floors that needed scrubbing, and carpets that needed vacuuming. The pair of them looked like a couple of convicts and were clearly sinking their teeth into the whole psychology. Their posture was hunched, their faces were white, and they were bonding in a way that only two prisoners can. It was a long day for those two knuckleheads, but the house was clean and I was standing proud and tall. Good job.

Victory was mine.

CHAPTER 2

A NOT-SO-GOOD FRIDAY

Maddy

The first time I stole, I was eight. I was at a grocery store with Lauren, who was a couple of years older than me. She basically considered me to be her living doll and would get me to act out and do all sorts of things. There was nothing she loved more than bossing me around.

One of my earliest memories is of her forcing her brother, Patrick, and me to get married. She planned the nuptials for days and even knew the color of underwear that she would have on. When she was nine and I was seven, Lauren decided that she was going to get really serious about religion. It just so happened that I was sleeping over on Good Friday when she decided that she would try to help me find God. She told me all about how Jesus had been crucified on that day.

"What does *crucified* mean?"

"It's when someone nails your feet and arms to a cross because you've done something bad," she explained.

"What did he do that was so bad?"

"He started to become really popular and his best friend sold him down the river."

I thought that maybe she had fallen off her rocker.

"Then why is it called *Good* Friday?" I asked.

"Just look out the window and sing your prayers to the stars," she instructed, obviously frustrated with my cross-examination.

I did it.

She then spent hours teaching me some song she had learned in her sign language choir at school. That's right, we sang the entire song with our hands. At around six in the morning we went downstairs to watch some television when Lauren found a made-for-TV movie about Jesus. We watched the whole thing, and I was traumatized by just how bloody the process was.

A year later (on what just happened to be a Friday), my mom decided to take Ian, Patrick, Lauren, and me grocery shopping with her. Mom instructed us to behave, like she always did when she let us loose in public. Lauren told my mom that she would watch me while Mom shopped. Mom agreed and went on her way. The moment Mom was out of sight, Lauren turned to me and told me that we were going to eat the candy in the bins. I knew that this wasn't right, but my lame protest was met with the promise that we wouldn't get caught, and she said she did it all of the time. Being a candy addict, I quickly threw my apprehensions to the way-side. Lauren showed me how to take candy from the bins and smoothly walk over to the canned goods, where we pretended to be looking for a certain item (like two eight-year-olds are buying canned goods). We stuffed the candy into our little mouths while standing there, examining the cans. We then put the cans back as though they were not exactly what we were looking for.

This went on for some time. I was so happy eating all that free candy that even though I knew I was doing something wrong, I didn't care. Everything was all fine and dandy except for the fact that my mom was watching us. Of course, I was unaware of this, seeing as how I was hopped-up from the candy. She let us do this for a while, until the time was right. She came up to us and asked what we were looking at. I slowly turned from the cans and confessed. "Nothing." She grabbed our grubby little hands, full of candy, and marched us over to the manager. Busted! How could my own mother turn me in? She explained to the manager that we had been stealing candy and then told her that she would completely understand if the police needed to get involved. My mind was racing a thousand miles a minute (thanks to the candy). My life flashed before my eyes. I imagined my future in jail and it didn't look good. I would be somebody's bitch in a matter of seconds, and how would I ever fit into one of those jumpers? They would have to get one custom-made. Would I ever see my bear, Big Blue, again? Maybe he could come? Letters were obviously out of the question since I couldn't read or write (I was a little slow). I searched for an answer to this awful predicament; then it came to me: I started crying like I had never cried before and pointed my candy-stained finger at the one person I knew would take the heat off of me. Lauren seemed less concerned than I was. We stood there at the counter and got completely messed with. I was certain that at any moment the police would show up and cuff us. I didn't understand how Lauren could be so calm while I was shaking uncontrollably. My mom turned to me and said, "I'm sorry, but the law is the law and you broke it. I just hope that I can visit you in jail." I couldn't believe it. One mistake and my life was ruined forever. I tried to imagine what I would do without my mom there to take care of me.

After a while of me thinking of my life surrounded by cement walls, the manager said she wouldn't call the police but that we would have to pay for what we had taken. My mom looked down at me and asked if I had any money to pay for it.

"Uh, no."

My mom thought for a moment and then said she was willing to pay for it but that she was doing us a huge favor and that the money would be paid back in full by both of us. We left the store and got into the car with the boys, who were laughing that we had gotten in trouble. My mom started driving and asked us if the candy was worth it. I shook my head no but debated with myself. The candy was pretty good.

When we got home the torture really started. My mom gave us a list of chores that she had drawn up. First we had to fold all of the laundry in the house. I had never done chores before and was mad that I had to start. I sat there with

Lauren, looking at pile upon pile of laundry. We started folding. I looked at Lauren and rued the day she had come into my life. I was mad that she had made me steal, and now I was paying the price. I was reminded of Cinderella and knew that there was no prince at the end of this tale. Cinderella had been good and wasn't a thief. Lauren sat there, unfazed by all of it. By the end of the day I was exhausted.

Any time my mom went back to that grocery store, I hated going with her because I was sure that one day the manager would change her mind and arrest me. Even going there with my dad was painful. I would instantly get shaky and embarrassed at what I had done. I still won't go into that place for fear of being recognized.

Imagine, my own mother was willing to sell me down the river for penny candy. I started to understand how Jesus must have felt and thanked God that nailing me to a slab of wood had never crossed my mother's mind.

Because surely stealing candy was far worse a crime than being popular.

CHAPTER 3

FRONT OF THE CLASS

Joan

Maddy has always been incredibly social, loving nothing better than a roomful of people all talking over one another (as is my family's way) and laughing. Right from the time she could talk, she wanted to socialize. When she found herself with too much free time, she would, without fail, get up to no good—like cut her hair or shave her legs (at the age of eight)—so it was never easy when things around the house were quiet. Ian, on the other hand, loved nothing more than an empty, quiet house so that he could really relax.

Maddy's sociableness got in the way of her schooling right from the very beginning. Her first report card from junior kindergarten (when four years old, for God's sake) focused on her inability to sit still. She was also accused of being disruptive and distracting the other kids from their "studies" with her antics and stand-up comedy routine.

A part of me felt secretly proud of the little gal. She was developing her personality and spreading her wings, but the reality was that she needed a good stern talking-to: no candy (her lifeline) and no *Wizard of Oz* (she knew every dance step and lyric).

Thus began Maddy's academic career. Trouble right out of the gate. Maddy's first teacher was great and was so taken with her that she really wasn't concerned. She and I were trying to keep the little filly under control. She had the same lovely teacher for senior kindergarten, and we continued trying to keep Maddy in check, but after all, it was only kindergarten.

In grade one, things started heating up. Maddy's new teacher was a strange duck. She was so unbelievably smitten with Maddy that she asked nothing from her. Not ideal. The kid was being taught that being a clown and an amazing conversationalist would be enough to get her through life. That would be fine if she decided she wanted to be a con artist for a living, but it wasn't going to fly in my house.

Miss J just couldn't say enough fine things about Maddy— but I kept asking why Maddy still couldn't tie her shoes or tell time. I know I should have been reading to the kids more regularly, but I just never seemed to have the time, and when I did, I couldn't see straight thanks to the constant fatigue that had set in. So of course I blamed myself for the fact that by grade one, Maddy couldn't read at all. On top of having a lousy mother, Maddy was going to be learning from ol' Miss J for a second year in the next grade. The school administration, not knowing that Maddy was on holiday with this teacher, placed her with Miss J for grade two. I think Miss J may have even requested to have Maddy again. I didn't switch Maddy out of the class because she just loved Miss J. It was a little crazy when I look back on it, but it seemed okay at the time. So Maddy spent another full year entertaining Miss J and the rest of her classmates and still learning absolutely nothing except how to tell a good knock-knock joke. Strangely, her report cards were always glowing, and Miss J couldn't say enough great things about this "magical" little girl.

Toward the end of that year, I decided it was time to sell the house. We had lived in a modest semidetached since a year before my husband and I split up. It was a fixer-upper—which is fine if you are married to a contractor (which my husband was at the time) but not ideal at all for a broke, newly single mother of two. I didn't do any fixing and wasn't taking any uppers, so the house was in its original condition for the first five years that we lived in it. We did the best we could with what we had and, all in all, it really wasn't that bad. As I told the kids endlessly, they could be living in an appliance box or in Afghanistan, so no hot-water tap in the kitchen was a breeze. The last couple of years we were there, I had managed to start turning my finances around—the talent agency was starting to make me some money, and I put every cent into the house. I soon had an apartment built in the basement, and just by luck, my lesbian cleaning woman and her girlfriend moved in. They were both tough as nails, so it saved me getting a security system. Even so, I woke up one morning and knew I had to reduce my stress level. Something had to go—I had to keep the kids, so that wasn't an option, and the business was just starting to make a profit, so that left the house. Two days later the place was sold and my lawyer figured out that I was going to be netting a whopping seven hundred Canadian dollars (which at that time was about five hundred U.S. dollars). Pretty lame really, but at least I didn't owe any money.

I decided to rent a house in a bit more of a swanky area, which meant the kids were going to have to change schools. Neither of them were too pleased. Ian was going to have to start grade five at the new school and Maddy, grade three. I wasn't worried about them since I thought they were young enough to adapt. The big bonus was the fact that the new school had an excellent reputation and was just one hundred yards from the new rental I had found. It was a really great old brownstone, and the kids and I loved it. Everything, I told myself, was going to be just fine.

Ian adapted quite nicely. He didn't love his teacher, but everything was going pretty smoothly with his schoolwork. Maddy, however, was having trouble. Her teacher's name was Mrs. K, and she was lovely but took no crap from any of the kids or their parents. The polar opposite of Miss J, Mrs. K was shocked by Maddy's inability to sit still and obey the rules. Within a week Maddy's seat was changed so that she had to sit right next to the teacher, a tradition that lasted pretty much all the way through Maddy's future years in school. It was always so embarrassing on Parents' Night. Without fail some nosy mother would ask where my daughter sat, and I would have to point to the lone desk in the front of the class next to the teacher's desk.

One Parents' Night, Mrs. K became extremely animated when she realized I was the mother of the devil-child herself. She explained, a little more loudly than I would have liked, that Maddy was completely and utterly out of control. I asked if maybe she thought this was due to the recent move, and Mrs. K shook her head furiously. She explained that there was no way this was new behavior and that Maddy was also sadly behind in her reading. I couldn't get out of there fast enough. I told Mrs. K that I would speak to Maddy and promised to stay on top of it. I suggested that we meet again in a month or so and discuss it further.

Unfortunately, things got worse. Maddy was getting more and more rowdy and forgetful. Half the time she came home, she was barefoot—how do you forget your shoes, and what are they doing off in the first place? I tried to read with her as much as possible, but without fail her book bag would be forgotten at school, at her dad's—or anywhere she could ditch it. Not good since her reading comprehension was almost nonexistent.

A month later when Mrs. K and I met formally to discuss Maddy's problems, I looked her straight in the face (a face I was growing to trust) and asked if Maddy was drowning. She said, "Yes, no question." Oh boy. I asked Mrs. K what level Maddy was at in her basic subjects, and she answered somewhere in the late grade one range. Oh my God—she was a full year and a half behind where she should have been. My gut told me right off the bat that she needed to be put back a year. She was born in December, so she wouldn't be that much older than her classmates, and she'd have a fighting chance at getting on top of her game. The switch wouldn't go unnoticed by her peers, though, which was going to be a problem for sure. I also needed to get some testing done to see if we were dealing with more than just the fact that Maddy had been holidaying with Miss J for two years. Maybe there was something bigger afoot.

Putting Maddy back a year was probably one of the biggest decisions I've ever had to make about the kids. It was agonizing. Everybody seemed to be split on the issue, including the school staff and the team of experts I had to meet with on the topic. Maddy's father was vehemently opposed, my mom was in favor, and it went on from there—but the bottom line was, as always, it came down to me. I spoke with Mrs. K several times and slowly discovered that she was behind me on this move, despite the fact that it wasn't fashionable at the time.

Anyway, it was becoming clear that Maddy had been causing trouble in class to divert attention from the fact that she didn't know how to do the work. The poor little darling—she was just trying to hang on to her pride. Such a dangerous thing.

I broached the subject of putting her back a year, and Maddy freaked out completely. How could I even suggest such a thing? Was I trying to completely ruin her life? Was I just really a monster? (My favorite.) I attended a definitive meeting at the school with the principal, Mrs. K, the school board's psychologist, the school board's social worker, the special-education teacher, and the vice principal. With the exception of Mrs. K, no one at the table really wanted to put her back, or so they said officially. I had the sneaking suspicion that a couple of them wanted to say "do it," but the official line at the time was that Maddy would pay a big emotional price. What they didn't know was that Maddy was made of strong stuff, and in spite of her insecurities around her academics, she was pretty damn confident in other areas. Also, both Mrs. K and I saw absolutely no way for her to catch up. That was the reality, and by the time we finished the meeting, I had the support of the team.

In the meantime, the team at the school had also concluded that Maddy needed "special attention." They recommended that we put her into the Learning Center on a daily basis to help her catch up on her reading and writing. It turned out she could not learn by rote and needed a visual and an explanation attached to anything she was expected to remember and/or learn. This didn't seem like anything too extreme; she would probably be diagnosed with attention deficit disorder or something along those lines if she were in today's system. So we set out to get the paperwork signed. Basic goals would be set. We would wrestle the problem to the ground.

The meeting was on Friday, and we decided there was no time like the present. On Monday, Maddy was going back to grade two.

When I explained to Maddy on Friday night that she would be going back to grade two on Monday, she was not surprised after the weeks of prepping—but still mighty angry. She was horrified at the prospect of being with the younger kids and was especially nervous about being pulled out of class every day to go to the Learning Center. She was embarrassed and very upset. Who wouldn't be? But I believed then, and still do, that there was no way she was going to make it at all if we just kept rolling along, pretending everything was okay when it wasn't.

She was unhappy and resentful for the first few weeks. Mothers can't always be popular, I was learning, but I still felt terrible for her. But after another couple of weeks, she was showing signs of recovery. She was more cheerful and was returning to her old self. She hated the Learning Center and hated it for the next few years to come, but the classroom was starting to be a bit more comfortable. She also was discovering that these kids looked up to her as an older, cooler kid, which of course she was going to milk for all it was worth. She was completely obsessed with sports and was turning into quite the swimmer and gymnast. Things were turning around.

What Miss Maddy didn't tell me until a bit later was that she, since then, has felt uncomfortable on her birthday. Without fail someone would ask why she was in a grade lower than she should have been. Also, the Learning Center, as good as it was, was probably not enough for her learning difficulties.

I was quickly realizing, contrary to my previous belief, that I wasn't going to be a general after all in this war. I was going to be a soldier fighting on the front line in the trenches.

Chapter 4

Left Behind

Maddy

Grade two was a hard one for me. Since kindergarten I had gone to school in an area that was not fancy. Most of the kids that went to the school were from blue-collar, working families like mine was at the time. People didn't have designer clothes, nor did they feel a huge want for them. My school went from kindergarten to grade eight, which made it one of the larger schools in Toronto. I did well in my classes, I could draw inside the lines and recite my ABCs, and I was well liked by teachers and students. Life was good.

I didn't know how to read by the time I was in grade two, but my teacher didn't seem to be concerned and neither was I. It wasn't until the end of grade two that my mom decided we needed an upgrade. Her talent agency was doing well, and she decided to rent a house in a better area where the schools were better and it was safer. I didn't want to leave my school, where I felt safe. I also didn't want to leave my crush. His name was Tyrone, and he was in grade eight. The guy must have been about six feet and had the most beautiful dark skin. I decided at a young age that white guys just weren't for me. There was no chance for me and Tyrone, but I was in grade two and didn't realize that. I would go up to him every recess and say hi, he would politely pat me on the head and say that I was cute. I thought that he was saying it in a romantic way, but in reality he was just saying I was a cute little kid. I was horrified that I would have to leave this budding relationship but knew I had no choice.

We moved at the end of the school year and were bought off by the gift of a puppy we named Harley. I stayed in touch with my friends but started making new ones in my new area. I quickly got over the move, as young kids do. When the fall came, I was ready to start my new school. Ian, who was going into grade five, was instantly popular as the new, hot thing at school. That made me the little sister of someone cool, which is always a plus. I went into my grade-three class and knew that I could win over the class and teacher with my colorful personality. I loved my new teacher, Mrs. K. She had art days every Thursday and was an encouraging, inspirational person. However, she didn't enjoy my disruptive personality—the constant talking, joking at the teacher's expense, and all the fun that I was creating for myself and the other students. I was quickly moved to a desk away from the other students, which was positioned against the wall, by the jackets on hooks. My desk faced the wall and when the door was left open, as it often was, I would be completely enclosed by the walls and the door. I didn't really let this get me down but always longed to be back with the group.

The demands placed on the students at my new school were much more severe than those at my previous institution. I was surprised to learn that all of the other students in my class had known how to read for some time and to discover that I was quite behind. Mrs. K spent much of her time trying to get me on track without much luck. I had learned that if I just acted out, it would overshadow my lack of intelligence. Mrs. K realized exactly what was going on. She had a meeting with my mom, and before I knew it, Mom sat me down with the news that I would be put from grade three back to grade two. I couldn't believe it. It seemed that everyone, including my dad, was against me. In what world would I want this to happen? Not only did I feel completely stupid, but I also felt embarrassed about being with the younger kids. Mom told me I had no choice in the matter and would be starting in my new class the following Monday. I had already been the new kid and was only one month into my new environment, but now I would also be the dumb kid. The news got worse. I would also have to start going to the Learning Center.

I went to school that Monday and entered my new class, which was directly across the hall from my old class. How was I going to explain to my old friends why I wasn't in that class anymore? Things could not have been worse. I sat on the carpet with my new younger classmates and tried to blend in.

The teacher, of course, wouldn't let that happen and told me to stand up and introduce myself. I did it but hated her for it. I didn't really talk to anyone the first day and sat at my group table longing for my private desk facing the wall in grade three. The next day I tried to make friends. I asked another little girl if she wanted to be my friend and she blatantly said no. The only friend I had was the girl who lived across the street. She was a weird kid, but beggars can't be choosers. I would go over to her house every day to play, and she would come up with strange games. She always tried to play games where she would kiss me. It was really uncomfortable. She explained that if she put on lip balm and then kissed me, it wasn't really kissing, as the balm was a barrier. Suffice it to say, I stopped playing with her.

The Learning Center wasn't any better. All of the kids seemed to have major issues. Some would scream, which made my behavior seem angelic. My reading didn't improve. I was even behind the grade-two students, and I knew it. My stepmom, Becky, had been a teacher and was pregnant with my little brother. She made cue cards and pronunciation charts and started my reading at the kindergarten level. I sat at that fucking dining room table hour after hour, crying out of frustration, sounding out the letters of the alphabet and eventually combining them. I sounded like an idiot. "T-t-t-h-h-h-h-e-e-e-e . . . the." The words might as well have been Chinese. Starting from square one when you're old enough to be self-conscious is an awful feeling. Becky was the only one I didn't want to kill when she tried to help me. She didn't get frustrated with me, and she created fun games that would make me forget the educational purpose. Without her I really don't know what I would have done. The school had already put the kibosh on my attempts to slip through the cracks of the education system. My mom had taken some time off to help me and watch the O. J. Simpson trial. I would sit at the dining room table trying to rap different spellings of words, with the trial on in the background. I managed to get through grade two but was scarred for the remainder of my educational career. I was always a little behind where I should have been.

The following year I was placed back in Mrs. K's third-grade class for round two. I continued going to the Learning Center, but I also continued acting out. I had reclaimed my seat facing the wall and felt at home. I had not really thought that I would have to explain every year that I was put back a grade, but when my birthday came around, I was forced to tell my fellow classmates why I was a year older. I knew that as soon as I told them, they would look at me differently, and that's the last thing I wanted to be—different. I grew to hate my birthday because I saw it as a reminder that I was dumb.

By the time grade four rolled around, I had become good at acting out in order to cover up my lack of intelligence. I thought that if I could just charm the students, they wouldn't see that I struggled with school. I put on a too-cool-for-school attitude early in the game. My teacher, Ms. R, knew me from reputation and decided to try and nip my behavior in the bud. In the class, she had reading groups: There was the high level, middle level, and low level. I was in the low level and was given skinny books with big letters while my friends had chapter books. I played it off well by saying that I was lucky because I didn't have to do as much work. Ms. R didn't make anything easier for me. Whenever the Learning Center called the classroom for me, good old Ms. R would yell over the entire class, "Maddy, it's time for you to go to the Learning Center." It was so humiliating.

One day we were all sitting on the carpet while Mrs. R began her math lesson. Naturally, I was behind in my math as well, and she knew it. I sat there as I did every day, playing with someone's hair and chatting, when she asked the class who would like to come up to the board and do a long-division question. She skipped right over all of the hands that were lifted and directed her gaze at me. "Maddy, why don't you come up here and do it?" she asked. I looked at her and said, "No, I don't want to." She insisted that I come up and do the question in front of the class. I got up, took the chalk from her hand, and stood with my back to everyone, panicking. I had no idea what to do. I couldn't start because I just didn't get it. She let me stand there for a good minute. "That's what I thought. You can't do it." I turned around with my face completely flushed. She started to laugh and then told me to sit down and pay attention. I went home that night and forced my dad to teach me long division. It took all weekend, but once it clicked, it clicked. I went back to school on Monday and looked forward to the math lesson. We all gathered on the carpet and Ms. R started the lesson. I raised my hand and asked if I might be allowed to do the long-division question. "We're past long division now," Ms. R said.

It was to become the story of my public-school career: always one step behind everyone else.

Chapter 5

Running on Empty

Joan

It was just another Saturday with the kids—one of those days when you take a look around the mess and the madness and decide that you've got to bust out of the house or risk someone's death. Ian was ten and Maddy was eight—the height of their combat days. There always seemed to be a conflict between them, which inevitably resulted in violence, and I just wasn't up for it that day. I decided that taking them to a movie would be the best way to distract everyone, including me. We loved going to movies together, and it was also a surefire way to get them to sit in one place for a couple of hours without any breakage, spillage, or punching. I have to say that even at their worst and rowdiest ages, I could almost always count on them to chill out for a couple of hours in a dark theater.

This was a particularly tough time for me financially. The

phone, electricity, and heat were cut off regularly. I was the queen of running out of gas in my car. People thought I was a flake, but the reality was that very often my paycheck from my struggling talent agency was ten or fifteen bucks. It's pretty hard to run a house and feed a couple of kids on that kind of revenue. In addition, my ex and I were in dispute about our financial arrangements, and my fancy-pants lawyer was charging me a fortune for nothing but double-talk. To add insult to injury, the kids' dentist had told me that both of them needed braces—another few grand—and on it went. Somehow in spite of this crazy financial situation, I was pretty cheerful—tired but cheerful—except, of course, for those odd times when I would just cry my head off over a beer with my friend Heather. It was during one of those crying jags that Heather and I decided that we would get our psych-ward preadmission papers in order just to speed things up on that one final day when things got to be too much. Heather's life wasn't a cakewalk at the time either, so we took care of each other and kept each other laughing.

Fortunately, during this time in our lives I wasn't on deck every weekend with the kids. They spent every other weekend with their dad, and I usually spent those weekends lying on the couch watching television and/or staring at the wall. These were years when I was running on empty. The weekdays were jammed with school, work, housework, and sports activities that I thought would make the kids better people. I still don't know if sports made them better people, but the activities sure as hell made me a tired, burned-out, single mother, so those weekends off were key for refueling. The refueling was usually effective, so "on" weekends were filled with outings that were as cheap as possible. Aside from movies, we enjoyed terrorizing the apple farm and the zoo.

One weekend I called Heather and asked if her two would be up for seeing *Homeward Bound*, a Disney story about a couple of pets that get lost in the wilderness and have to find their way back home. Heather jumped on the chance to have an afternoon away from her kids. I drove over and picked them up and brought along one of Maddy's friends as well. What's five kids?

I, for some unknown reason, was always the one to take out a group of kids and show them a good time. The outings almost always ended in tears, but they say pain doesn't have a memory. I signed up again and again like a glutton for punishment.

After the movie, which the kids loved, we squeezed into my beloved, newly acquired, ten-year-old Honda that couldn't make it up hills. The radio was broken, so Maddy would sing anything I wanted to hear, from country western to rap. She was a terrific entertainer but not that day. The kids were completely out of control during the car ride home, with the exception of Lauren, who was in the front seat with me. The backseat crew was playing some invented game that involved hitting each other harder and harder. With each punch or slap the screaming got louder. I was starting to really lose it, and screaming over their screams wasn't going to cut it. I threatened to throw them out of the car like my mother had done to us when we were wrestling in the car. The point I missed with this particular form of punishment was that my mother did it when we were staying at our cottage, where there were no criminals on the country roads. Crackheads didn't even exist yet—it was the early sixties, for God's sake. After several warnings, I pulled the car over and threw the four culprits out of the car.

Of course I was planning to circle the block and pick them right back up, but they deserved a scare. I had done this a number of times before and it always worked like a charm. The kids ranged in age from eight to ten, with Ian being the oldest.

I pulled up about three minutes later to the spot where I had left them. I confess that although it wasn't the worst area of town, it certainly was not the best.

There was no sign of them.

It was the same feeling you get when your car is towed—you wonder if maybe you left it somewhere else and if you might be just a little confused. After about ten minutes of looking all over the immediate area, Lauren, who had been good and was still in the car with me, started to cry and asked if she was ever going to see her little brother again. Jesus, this was not good. I had visions of myself splattered all over the front pages as the first person to not only lose a group of kids but to have also deliberately thrown them to the wolves. I decided to drive to the nearby mall, where I asked the manager to announce their names over a loudspeaker—nothing. Panic was really starting to kick in and there were no cell phones in those days, so I headed to the pay phones with a nearly hysterical Lauren. The least I could do for that family was try to keep their one remaining child alive.

I called the police and they arrived at the mall a few minutes later. While I waited, I called my friend Heather and explained that I had dumped the kids and that they had somehow vanished. Heather couldn't go too crazy on me because she was also a proponent of throwing the kids out of the car and had done it herself a number of times. It was just the part about her son being lost that made her a wee bit upset. The cops arrived and drove Lauren and me around in the back of the cruiser and scoured the streets—all to no avail. The police thought this was all pretty damned funny. They assured me that it was highly unlikely that someone would bother abducting four kids and that they were probably just on their way home. I explained that they knew the drill because I had done this a number of times before and that they would never ever step this far out of line. Then I thought that I could just drive my Honda off a bridge and send everyone involved a very big letter of apology. What else could I do?

Heather stayed cool as a cucumber and joined us in the search for the missing kids. Like me, she didn't really have any answers as to where the hell they had gone, but if they were alive, they were in deep shit. We tried calling our homes again and again but no answer. A couple of hours went by and I could tell the police were getting a little tired of the search. They believed that not only were the kids fine but that also I was learning one hell of an important lesson: Don't throw my kids out of the car.

Finally, after much hand wringing and searching and crying, Heather tried calling her house one last time. Ian answered.

Relief! Heather, Lauren, and I ran over to Heather's.

When I heard the tale of their own homegrown version of *Homeward Bound*, I was not only furious but also incredibly embarrassed by my own failure to keep the kids safely out of the way of every lunatic in the city. Even though I was more pissed at myself than at Ian, I could under no circumstances show weakness to the kids and let them have victory. That night I made Ian write a letter of apology to everyone involved, much to his protests—after all, he was taking the position that I had created the whole situation and he had reacted like any good Boy Scout would. I probably should have taken a page from his lesson book. It was clearly time for me to take a closer look at myself and pull it together.

CHAPTER 6

HOMEWARD BOUND

Maddy

I'm not usually a fan of movies that feature talking animals, but when my mom took Ian, Lauren, Patrick, Sarah, and me to *Homeward Bound*, I thought it was inspiring. These helpless domestic animals braved the wild and against all odds found their way home. Seeing as how we had been sitting quietly like angels for two hours in the theater while eating a copious amount of sugar, when we all piled into the car to head home, we were a bit revved up. We weren't doing anything particularly bad in the backseat, but I remember my mom yelling nevertheless. We did what all kids do: squish into each other at every turn and play tag (basically just hitting each other as hard as we could). Apparently we went over the line while playing a rousing game of throw things out the car window, a game we all enjoyed. The object of the game was to throw whatever we found out the window and try to muffle our laughter. When Ian threw my doll out the window, however, I screamed in horror. This is when my mom snapped. She pulled over the car and told Ian, Patrick, Sarah, and me to get out. We looked at her for a minute trying to decide if she was serious.

"GET OUT!!!!"

We determined that she was in fact serious and did as she demanded. As we watched her speed off with Lauren still in the car, we all stood there a little baffled. That's when Ian decided he would have to take over the situation. Because he was ten and I was only eight, I usually listened to him.

"Okay. Well, we better start walking if we are going to get home before dark."

I wondered if he had completely lost his mind.

"Ian, she's coming back."

I had already survived multiple getting-kicked-out-of-the-car incidents and felt pretty confident that Mom was coming back. After all, not all of us belonged to her. The first time I had been kicked out, she drove only a few feet away, and every time thereafter she would drive a little farther than the last. After about five minutes my confidence started to crumble, and that's when Ian started to make sense. He convinced us that if we followed him, he could lead us home. We weren't in the best neighborhood, and being there at night wasn't something I wanted to experience. As we started walking from our drop site, I kept looking back, hoping that I would see Mom's car and we could all have a good laugh, but she never showed up. I tried to walk slowly but knew if I didn't follow Ian, I would be completely on my own. There were four of us; we had strength in numbers. We walked toward what looked like a strip mall, thinking someone there could tell us where we were and what we needed to do to get ourselves home. Just like the animals in the movie, we were innocent creatures left to fend for ourselves in the urban wilderness. The strip mall turned out to be an Asian market. Not one sign was written in English. We walked around the market for a half hour before deciding that this place was not going to be the salvation that we first thought, and then we listened to Ian's next plan of action.

Sarah's Mom had given her money for the movie, which my mom hadn't accepted, so we had a resource. Ian decided that we would walk until we found a place to buy a map and some water—dehydration was a concern of his—and then we would map out the best route home and possibly take public transportation. I had to hand it to him—his plan made sense. We walked and walked and walked some more. When we finally found a store, we were all pretty excited. We walked in and bought a map, water, and a few candies for the road. After Ian examined the map, it was clear that walking was out of the question. We would have to take a bus, the subway, and another bus. Our journey was far from over.

Ian was quite short for his age and looked to be about eight, like the rest of us. We knew that people on the transit system would look at us oddly since we were not with an adult, so we would have to come up with a good reason why we were on our own. We were mad at Mom for abandoning us, but we weren't mad enough to tell the truth about our sad situation. We knew that if anyone heard about what she had done, an investigation into her parenting might take place. It was clear she didn't care about our well-being, but we had our dignity and didn't want to sink to her level. Ian came up with a plan that was pure genius. If anyone asked, we would tell them we were all brothers and sisters who played on a competitive basketball team and we were going to the Y for a game. Thinking about it now, I realize it sounded a little far-fetched. Ian was short, I was chubby, Patrick looked like he couldn't even lift a ball let alone throw one, and Sarah was tiny. She was also Spanish. The four of us waited for the bus. The fare emptied our pockets. While on the bus we had to decide whose house we were going to go to—our house or Lauren and Patrick's house. It made more sense to go to Patrick's house because my mom wouldn't be there.

The bus ride was uneventful. We got to the subway station and boarded the train, trying to look like we had done it a hundred times before. I started talking really loudly, "SO, REMEMBER YESTERDAY WHEN WE WERE ON THE SUBWAY? YEAH, THAT WAS A GOOD SUBWAY RIDE." I had not yet learned the art of subtlety. My brother cut me the look of "you're an idiot," so I shut up. We were almost at our stop when an elderly lady came up to us and asked where our parents were. Right away I launched into the story that we were all siblings on a competitive basketball team and we were headed to the Y. Now, I could have ended the story there, but for some reason I felt it needed more. I started talking about how I balanced my basketball career with a gymnastics career. I continued with the statement that I hoped to be competing in gymnastics on behalf of Canada in the 2000 Olympic Games. She looked at me and smiled; I think she thought I was handicapped, so she patted me on the head and turned away. Ian leaned over and whispered into my ear, "You're stupid, shut up." I pouted for the remainder of the ride but lost all memory of my brother's harsh words the moment we got to our stop.

The next leg of our journey was to take another bus. Ian seemed to know where we were and decided we could walk it. After my encounter with the old lady, he also thought that we should avoid public transportation at all costs. I still had no idea where we were and put all of my trust in Ian. We walked for what seemed like forever. I don't like to think of myself as a whiner, but I have been known to belt out a few high-pitched complaints when necessary. Not only was I physically tired, but I was also emotionally drained. I had just been abandoned by my very own mother. The one person in the world who was supposed to protect me from the harsh realities of the street had thrown me deliberately into them. Finally I whined, "Are we there yet?" Ian, never taking his eyes off the road that lay ahead, simply said, "Home is right over that hill." I knew that I had heard that line somewhere before, and then it clicked—it was a direct quote from *Homeward Bound*. But when the wise dog said that to the cat and the cheeky dog, he was wrong. Their home was not over the hill. In fact, when they got to the top of that hill there were just more damn hills.

I was at my breaking point when I recognized a convenience store. I had bought Lick-a-Made there only days earlier. At that moment, I stepped in front of the pack and led the lost children home. When we finally got to the house, we were pretty proud of ourselves. No one was there, which by this time didn't surprise us. We looked at the clock to see how long our never-ending journey had indeed taken us and realized that we had been on the road for only an hour and a half. We turned on the TV and waited for an adult to surface and congratulate us on getting ourselves home safe and sound. When the phone rang, Ian answered it. It was Patrick's mom. She said that she and Mom would be there shortly. When Ian got off the phone, he said that he felt like trouble was coming our way. This caught me a little off guard. How could they be mad when my mom was the one who had forced us into this situation?

The moment they walked in the door, they breathed a sigh of relief that we were fine—before exploding. Lauren, who had been with my mom the whole time, ran up to Patrick, crying with relief that we weren't dead. My mom said that she had called the police and had been in the cop car looking for us ever since. I elbowed Ian in the side and looked at him with that "I told you she would come back" stare. I knew the only way that I wouldn't be in trouble was to tell Mom that Ian had forced us to go with him and told us there was no way she would be coming back. Ian was in a lot of trouble. He was forced to apologize not only to Patrick's parents but also to Sarah's parents, who, when they allowed their little girl to go to a movie, didn't expect that she would be hunted down by the police as a missing child. I completely abandoned my brother and left him to take all responsibility, anything to stay out of trouble. Ian was in tears by the end of his reaming, but Lauren brought up a valid point: that it was smart of him to buy the map, at least. Somehow my mom did not find comfort in the fact that her son had street smarts. Instead, she asked how we had paid for the map, and when we told her with Sarah's money, Mom paid her back for the map and the other staples. We were ready to be mad at my mom for putting us up a creek without a paddle, but she somehow turned it around on us.

Instead of admitting that maybe she shouldn't have kicked us out of the car, she was mad that we didn't wait. Maybe she was mad that her lesson had backfired? Maybe she was afraid that she had lost control? All I know is that after that day, she never kicked us out of the car again. And, even if she had, we were always going to find our way home again.

CHAPTER 7

DOG-DAY AFTERNOON

Joan

I never wanted a pet of any kind, especially a dog. It's not that I don't like them. I'm allergic to them and that's all there is to it, but that didn't stop Ian and Maddy from wanting one. Maddy launched her "I want a dog" campaign when she was about three or four and did not let up until I finally caved in when she was six. Ian was no less keen on the acquisition—one of the few times brother and sister actually agreed on something.

A friend's dog had had a litter, and in a moment of weakness, I thought to myself, *Would it really kill me to do something that would make them happy?* After all, they had promised they would take care of the dog. I set up a time to get the Maltese/Lhasa apso puppy, then known as E.T., while the kids were at school. If I was going to go this far out on a limb, I might as well get the thrill of surprising them.

The little girl puppy was just gorgeous, but, not surprisingly, gave me a rash within a few minutes of my arrival. Regardless, when I got her home she began sliding all over the ceramic floor, and I fell in love. The kids were going to freak.

And freak they did. They walked in the door and knew something was up—probably because I was in an unusually good mood and hadn't ordered them to get to their homework (not that they ever obeyed that order). They turned the corner into the dining room, and there was their new baby staring at them. It was worth the forthcoming asthma attacks and chronic colds just to see their faces light up like never before. THEY LOVED HER!

Unfortunately, the kids had to leave a couple of hours later to go to their dad's for the night, so little E.T. and I were left on our own. This marked the beginning of yet another dysfunctional relationship in my life. The little monster barked until I wanted to cry, so I finally let her come into my bed. That was the end of the crate and any kind of proper training for the little beast. I couldn't resist her, though. The kids and I decided her name was not "right," so we changed it to Harley— a name suggested by one of the actresses I represented through my talent agency. She was a biker chick when she wasn't doing nonspeaking roles on TV commercials—and the name fit the puppy perfectly, so it stayed.

Harley lived with us for the next two and a half years, terrorizing the kids and anyone else who tried to come near her. The kids, needless to say, almost never walked her unless they were showing off and quickly invented their own special ways of torturing her. Maddy, a *Wizard of Oz* fanatic, thought of Harley as Toto, but Harley wanted none of the theatrics. This dog was *not* interested in being put in the basket on Maddy's bike or being held while Maddy belted out "Over the Rainbow." Harley would look at Maddy like she was a complete idiot. Ian took a much quieter approach—he'd take her up to his room and not let her out. All she wanted was to sit on my lap, eat cheese, and sit in judgment of my offspring.

Over the course of Harley's life at our house, she escaped several times only to land at the pound. After a couple of visits the employees knew her by name. She had bitten the kids countless times, but who could really blame her? They just wouldn't back off and leave her to digest her food and relax. Really, I could relate. I probably would have taken the odd nip at them if it were allowed.

The other problem with Harley was that she was making me sick—literally. I had a cold all the time. After the first year of Harley running the house and ruining my health, I suggested that we give her to a better home—maybe on a farm. Not that I knew anyone on a farm, but it sounded good. Each time I broached the subject, the kids looked at me as though I were just disgraceful. What did they care that I couldn't breathe and they never took care of her?

We had moved out of the house with ceramic floors and into a house with carpet. I had, in an attempt to save my sanity, shut down the agency and was basically lying around watching the O. J. Simpson trial and doing grade-two homework with Maddy until I figured out what I wanted to do with the rest of my so-called career. The bottom line was that Maddy needed some undivided attention from her mom. Also, after six years of catering to actors, I needed to rest. Not only were my allergies out of control, but also Harley was crapping and peeing all over the carpet. The house was a rental, and I could not afford to pay damages.

I have tried to live by the philosophy that the mark of a good soldier is to know his enemy's weaknesses. I have often waited for just the right moment of the kids' vulnerability to strike. Fortunately, Ian was just starting junior high and shifting his attention away from us (including from Harley), so I felt like the time was coming where I could get away with ditching the dog without him totally freaking out. Maddy, on the other hand, was a different story. She was a girl who loved her dog and no way was she giving her up. We'd see about that.

Not long after we moved into the new place, Maddy and Ian were visiting their dad for the weekend, and I got a frantic call from their stepmother saying that Maddy had been hurt. Maddy's dad had rushed her to the hospital after she had taken a tumble while tobogganing. Of course Miss Evel Knievel Jr. had had to tackle the big hills. She had broken her arm in a couple of places and went back to her dad's in quite a bit of pain. Maddy, much like myself, does not cope well with any kind of discomfort. I have always maintained that a paper cut can ruin my day, and she is no different. I braced myself for Precious's return the next day. Luckily, the O. J. trial was taking a weekend break.

Maddy came home wearing a look of pained martyrdom.

Imagine Joan of Arc and you start to get the idea. I always like to think there is a silver lining in every dark, miserable storm cloud, and sure enough, this time the lining was looking mighty silvery indeed. You see, Maddy was a bit groggy from the pain medication and was pretty much confined to the couch or her bed. SHE WAS WEAK. A rare and beautiful thing. I set about taking this opportunity to ditch our little darling Harley once and for all. Ian's friend from school had grandparents that were looking around for a small dog to provide them companionship. The stars were definitely lining up for me. I just had to get Maddy on board.

When I tried to calmly and lovingly explain that the dog was better off without us and that Harley could have a great, spoiled life with the elderly couple, she looked like she could have spit at me. Think Linda Blair in *The Exorcist*. Having been on her back for a few days had turned her hair into a total rat's nest at the back of her head. She called me a terrible person and screamed that I was ruining her life, which, thanks to her injury, was in the toilet already. Why would I hit her when she was down?

Over the course of the next couple of torturous days, Maddy held her puppy pretty close in spite of her extreme pain; all the while shooting me looks of total disgust and distrust. I guess she thought that if she just held on to Harley, I wouldn't be able to take her away. What she didn't know was that I was moving Harley's transfer forward at lightning speed. The elderly couple was thrilled at the prospect of getting this darling little dog. I neglected to tell them that she was not trained and that she bit children. They didn't have kids, so I didn't think that would be a problem. I was sad that we had to give her up, but I wasn't going to die for her.

Once things were finalized and the pickup day was established, I returned to the lair that Maddy had built for herself during her convalescence. The living room might as well have been a hospital room except the part where she had about a billion dollars worth of candy from all her visitors. She really was looking like hell, and the pain just wasn't subsiding. I figured I would deal with her physical pain once I got past the emotional injury I was about to inflict.

Thank God that Maddy was on the painkillers and had the broken arm, because I honestly think she would have come at me with both fists flying when I told her the dog leaving was a done deal. She sobbed, screamed, and ranted, but eventually, thanks to the meds, just ran out of steam and slept. It was during this little break that I got all of Harley's stuff organized. When Maddy woke up, her eyes were swollen and her face was blotchy. I felt bad, but there was no way around it.

The day came for Harley to be picked up and Maddy was as blue as you can get. Ian, on the flip side, was taking it like a champ. He actually understood that this whole dog thing wasn't for us and that we were probably not the best dog owners in town. He also got that I was probably going to die from the allergies and we were going to be evicted thanks to Harley's "accidents" on the rug.

After a very tearful good-bye to Harley, Maddy howled like a woman mourning the loss of her child. Now, please note,

I'm no coldhearted monster. I understand that separating a girl from her puppy is pretty tragic. However, self-preservation was quickly becoming the name of the game. And since it was clear that no one was going to adopt ME, I needed to forgive myself and soldier on.

CHAPTER 8

OVER THE RAINBOW

Maddy

My mom knew that it would be a challenge to make Ian and me happy about moving from one school to another but thought that buying us the puppy we had always wanted would soften the blow. On our last day at our old school she picked us up and took us to our new home. She told us that there was a surprise waiting for us. When we walked in the door, my mom knelt on the ground and slapped her hands on the floor. "Come here, E.T.!" The cutest little dog came running up to her. I had finally gotten my Toto. I was obsessed with *The Wizard of Oz* from the time that I can remember and had always wanted a little dog of my own to hold in my arms while singing about the land just over the rainbow. We quickly renamed her Harley, and she and I were inseparable for a time. The dog was cute but she would go to the bathroom wherever she saw fit and listened to no one. She did, however, help me make friends. We would go for walks to the park, which is where I met Nat in grade three. I used to really enjoy eating iced-tea powder, and I would sneak a ziplock bag of the stuff out of the house, using Harley as an excuse to leave. I would then retreat to the playground where I would sit behind the fence and eat my sugar. Nat and I found a common interest in this activity and became friends over iced tea. I became known as the girl with the dog and the powdered iced tea at the park.

The first time Harley ran away, I was up all night crying and making posters for her reward. We eventually found her at the animal shelter. By the third time she ran away, nobody really even looked for her as we knew someone would call and return her. She liked to escape and find some kind person who would give her a bath and feed her good food. She basically ran the show. My mom was the only one she really liked. I guess because I tortured her by making her wear doll clothes. All I wanted was for her to love me like my friends' dogs loved them, but with Harley I had no luck. If I tried picking her up while she was sleeping, I ran the risk of her biting me so hard that my skin would break. If I tried touching her while she was eating, the same thing would happen. The only time that it was actually safe to play with her is when she would come to me, which was rare. The dog that I had always wanted turned out to want nothing to do with me. Dorothy didn't have this problem with Toto. Harley and I had a love-hate relationship. She hated me and I loved her.

By the time grade four rolled around, nothing had changed.

Harley was still peeing all over the place and biting anybody she wanted. I could tell that my mom was getting sick of her, but I protested anytime she would even begin to suggest that Harley move out. By Thanksgiving, Harley had been trained and untrained. We had gone out of town for a while and had a woman stay with Harley who managed to train her to pee and poop outside, but a week into us being back, she had become untrained as a result of us not keeping up with the schedule.

One day I went to my dad's for a dinner with our extended family. My cousin Trish and I were a little too rowdy to be inside, so my Dad suggested that we go tobogganing. He helped us pull out the metal toboggan and greased it up so that it would be sure to fly. Trish and I had the option of two parks. We decided on the one farther away since it had a better hill. We got to the top of the hill, where we decided on a fine-looking path. A little over to our right, a jump had been built, but we decided that we would take a practice run before we went off the jump. We loaded ourselves onto the sled. I was in front and tucked my legs under the front rim, which curved up. Trish sat behind me and shoved us off. The greased-up, metal toboggan flew down that hill. I could see us veering toward the jump at a dangerous speed, but there was not enough time for me to bail, so I flew over the jump. While in the air I could hear some kid at the top yell, "Coooooool."

I landed and instantly had the wind knocked out of me. I couldn't move. Blood started pouring out of my mouth because I had bitten my tongue during impact. Trish ran over to me, laughing. I told her that I couldn't get up and that I thought that maybe I had broken my back. She panicked and asked me to get on the sled so that she could drag me home. I knew that I wouldn't be able to do that and instructed her to get my dad. She left me lying there and ran home. I lay there as a crowd gathered around me. By this time I was in complete shock. A woman who explained that she was a nurse talked to me while I lay in the snow waiting for my dad. My mouth was still bleeding and I was spitting up the blood. My dad seemed to be taking an awfully long time, and when he finally arrived, he explained that he had gone to the wrong park. The nurse told him that my back was probably fine, but my right arm was a different story. I hadn't even looked at my arm, but when I did, I started crying. There was a huge bump and my arm was all twisted. She said that I most likely snapped one of the two bones and that it was trying to poke through the skin. My dad got me up as the crowd clapped. My uncle had brought the car around to the park, and my dad got me into it. I remember how every bump in the road resulted in excruciating pain.

We got to the hospital and they took me right away. I lay on a gurney as they cut my favorite shirt off of my arm. I got an IV and went in for my X-ray. The nurse at the park was right. I had broken the main bone in my arm, right in half. The doctor told my dad that I would have to go into surgery. We decided that putting me under would be better than giving me painkillers. More of a sure thing. Right before I went in, I asked the nurse if I would be able to compete in my upcoming swim meet. She said that there was no way that I would be able to.

I was brought into the operating room, where they transferred me from the stretcher to the operating table. I thought, *I could get used to this sort of treatment—my feet haven't hit the ground all day.* They put a mask over my face and told me to count backward from one hundred. I started at one hundred and concentrated really hard on the number that followed. I didn't want to screw up the sequence and look dumb in front of all these people. I felt like I was taking a test. I think I passed out around eighty-seven.

When I started to come to, everything seemed like a dream. The nurse was talking in a low, slow-motion kind of way, which creeped me out, so I turned my head to look at my dad, who also tripped me out. I looked at my arm and saw a huge white cast that went up to my shoulder, forcing my arm into a bent position. I was groggy for hours but was feeling pretty damn good on all of the drugs. I was told that I would have to stay overnight at the hospital. My dad stayed with me the whole time. When I had to go to the bathroom, my dad carried me, as I was in no way steady on my feet. It made me a little embarrassed, but I had no choice. I didn't sleep well with the monitor beeping all night.

The next morning my mom came to the hospital. She had been talking to my dad the whole time I had been in the hospital, but they saw no need for both of them to be there. When I was released, we went back to my mom's house. Harley found it quite annoying that I had to take over my mom's bed and the couch. My mom's friend Heather and my aunt Kim came over that day and brought me candy and magazines. I hadn't even thought of that perk to getting hurt. I was still feeling a little weird from all of the painkillers I was on, so I decided to save my candy until later, which I never did. I lived for candy, so when I didn't dive right in, my mom knew I was in bad shape.

I woke up later that day to see that my candy had been moved. I asked where it was and found out that Ian had eaten all of it. What a bastard. I never really forgave him for that. I couldn't sleep, and the painkillers weren't helping. My arm started to throb and felt like it was going to explode. I went down to where my mom and the ladies were. I was crying in pain. My mom told me to try lying down on the couch. As I turned, the room erupted with laughter. I couldn't believe that they would be laughing at a time like this. I was dying. When I whipped around, they told me that they weren't laughing at my pain but at the rat's nest that had formed in my hair.

The pain didn't subside, so finally my mom took me back to the hospital. They said that the cast had been put on too tight and that my arm was swelling underneath it. They took me back to a small room where they pulled out an electric saw and went at the cast. I could feel the saw going into my arm and told them to stop. They didn't listen. I looked at my mom and asked her to make them stop. She didn't even acknowledge my request. "How can you let them do this to me!"

As it turned out, the saw wasn't going into my arm, but it felt like it. They recast my arm and sent me on my way.

My arm didn't hurt as much, but I still had to take a week off from school. Ian somehow convinced Mom that he, too, should stay home so that he could help me while she was working. He went to the video store with a specific order from me, but of course returned with not one of my movie requests. Instead, he rented action movies and video games that I couldn't operate. I tried to play with Harley, but she wanted nothing to do with me.

My hair had gotten so out of control that it now stood up on its own. There was talk of perhaps having to cut it. My mom went to the drugstore and bought three hot-oil treatments. I couldn't shower with the cast and was still too weak to give myself a bath, so my mom sat behind me on the couch and tried to deal with the mess in my hair.

"Listen, honey, we need to talk about Harley. We need to give her away. I'm allergic to her."

I hadn't said anything but she threw up defenses.

"Do you want me to be sick?"

I sat there, my head jerking back with every stroke of the brush, and didn't even attempt to put up a fight.

"Yeah, okay."

My mom couldn't really believe I was so cool with it. At that point, I honestly would have been okay with her giving me away.

It didn't take long to find Harley a home. One of Ian's friends had grandparents that were in the market for a dog. Before I could even come out of my haze, Harley was gone.

A few years later when I entered high school, I ran into Ian's friend. I asked how Harley was, and she told me a tale of the perfect dog. She was trained, didn't bite, and was super social. I asked her if she was talking about the same dog, and she confirmed that, yes, in fact, it was Harley, our little Maltese/ Lhasa apso. Harley by this time must have been eight years old. I was surprised she hadn't run away. I couldn't decide if it was the dressing-her-up part, or the locking-her-in-my-room part, but whatever it was, I guess she just didn't like our family. And although I sometimes felt like my mother was the Wicked Witch of the West, the truth was, I was Dorothy without a Toto.

Chapter 9

Enemy Lines

Joan

When I first started working for a fancy New York company, I was responsible for making sure that Teletubbies made it onto the right television networks in Canada and that we signed with the right companies to manufacture the stuff that would bear the Teletubbies' name and image. The Teletubbies were marching across the Atlantic and taking North America by storm, so life got crazy. Little did I know that this would mark the beginning of me becoming a part-time parent.

The kids were thirteen and fifteen and probably never needed me more. But we also had a ton of personal debt, and I had not been able to make enough money to support the family since leaving the talent agency behind. This was my big chance to give our family some financial security. My mom was getting a bit tired of lending me money.

I had never been part of anything that was so huge and creating such a stir internationally. Everybody wanted in on the action, and I was working twenty-four-hour days.

I remember my first business trip to Montreal with my boss, Dean. I left the kids with my assistant, Suzanne, who had become not just the brains of the business but also a surrogate mother while I was away. This was my first trip with Dean and was the beginning of our most excellent friendship. We hung out in the hotel, had beers, and talked about everything under the sun.

One of our topics of conversation was men and the type I should be looking for in my life. We both agreed the guy of my dreams would have to be a bit offbeat but really special and, of course, good-looking. Maybe a rich hippie or something.

The morning after our evening at the hotel, Dean and I headed to a meeting and, as luck would have it, in walked a gorgeous specimen of man wearing dirty clothes and a bike helmet. He looked like a cross between Antonio Banderas and Mel Gibson, with long, thick, brown hair, dark brown eyes, and a smile that blew my mind. He was so out of place in this corporate office that Dean and I couldn't take our eyes off him. We were introduced and I stared at him as though he were a movie star. To add to the fun, he spoke with a French accent! Even though he hung out for only a few minutes, Dean was convinced he was the man of my dreams. Our hosts explained, after he left, that they were sponsoring a portion of his round-the-world bike ride for charity.

It turns out Bike Guy (as he became known to us), had

been riding a bicycle around the world for four years. Now, most people, upon hearing this, would probably respond with "what a loser," but Dean and I, being a couple of saps, decided that he was downright heroic. The purpose of Bike Guy's quest was to raise money for a children's charity. He was noble and he was gorgeous. I quickly offered up my help, to our hosts, to contribute to Bike Guy's fund-raising. I wanted this guy as my boyfriend. Our hosts promised that they would have him get in touch with me and that I could take it from there. I'm quite sure they knew what I was really up to, but they were polite enough to go along with the pretense of me being a charitable human being.

A few weeks later I was in my home office doing the usual stuff—working, screaming at the kids between phone calls, and trying desperately to get them to "pretend" that they were doing some schoolwork.

Maddy was officially a teenager and had suddenly become very affectionate with me. She loved nothing more, for instance, than climbing into bed with me and stroking my head—she honestly thought we were married. I rationalized that it was better that she was stroking my head, and not some creepy teenage boy's. The only glitch with our new arrangement, I soon discovered, was that it was about to get in the way of my real love life (such as it was).

When Bike Guy called and said he was riding his bike home to Toronto from Montreal as part of the across-Canada final leg of his four-year journey, Maddy was very suspicious and, like others in my life, was not buying into my whole charitable shtick. She was adamant that I was trying to get with this guy and asked me since when did I have a passion for finding the cure for pediatric AIDS? That hurt, but I couldn't deny that, yes, I did want to date this guy. If I could get some money together for his cause at the same time, what the hell was wrong with that? The personal becomes the political, and all that.

Maddy (a.k.a. my wife) was none too pleased when Bike Guy rolled (literally) into town and arrived needing a shower (obviously, since he had ridden four hundred miles), a hot meal, and a cold beer—all things I was more than happy to provide. There had been a lapse of two weeks since I had made arrangements for him to stay at the house, so I had been on a crash diet and had been using the treadmill as something other than a clothes hanger. I thought I looked pretty good, but when I saw this Adonis walk in the door, I realized what being in shape really looked like—this guy was very seriously gorgeous and humble and hot. Or so it appeared.

Bike Guy wound up spending a couple of weeks at our house, adding to the circus atmosphere and pissing off my dear wife, Maddy. She was none too pleased with this guy and was outraged at my two-timing ways. She was going to make me pay. I, however, was over the moon—Bike Guy and I were forging a beautiful relationship and his imminent departure (on his bike) was making things all the more romantic and tragic. This, of course, made me just crazy about him—"always want what you can't have" was becoming my dating mantra.

Bike Guy and I had absolutely nothing in common and the most basic conversation was a stretch, but that didn't get in my way. I had raised a couple of thousand dollars for his cause through some of my corporate connections and had also managed to get him on a national news broadcast (which was filmed outside my house with Bike Guy on his bike). What I didn't realize at the time was that people were only doing me favors because they wanted in on the Teletubbies action. Those cute kids' characters were bringing out the greed in people.

Bike Guy and I were falling hard—or so I thought—and I was dreading the day he had to hop back on his bike to ride the three thousand miles or so to get to the West Coast. I, on the other hand, had a hard time getting up and down the stairs in my house. Maddy, meanwhile, was counting down the hours. In spite of the fact that Bike Guy and I took her to a huge carnival, to dinner, and anywhere else we could think of to remove the scowl from her pubescent face, she wasn't caving. One day we went over to my mom's pool to hang out, and in keeping with Maddy's theory that "constant vigilance will minimize the damage," she came along. She behaved so badly that I wanted to take her by the hair and toss her into the pool. Pure belligerence—and in front of my mom! She challenged every word that came out of my mouth and looked at me with such contempt, I wanted to cry out of frustration and rage.

Later I found out that my mom took Precious aside and, in the way only my mother can, shut her down with just three little words and a whole pile of attitude. "Cut it out." Maddy apparently had not bargained for Mom to side with me on the issue of Bike Guy the Imposter, which, by then, Maddy was convinced he was. My mother was having none of it and asked

Maddy point-blank if she wanted me to be alone for the rest of my life. Naturally, Maddy wanted to answer "YES!" but she could see that was not the right tack with her Nanna.

Maddy wasn't backing down though, and the evening after the swim, she was becoming more feral by the minute. I was edgy since I never knew when I would see her lurking in a corner just WATCHING. During the next couple of days when she did manage to get me cornered alone, she told me that Bike Guy was a phony schmuck and that he was completely using me. This was all capped off with, "You are making a complete fool of yourself." She was really busting my Zen with her vitriol. Was it so wrong that I was trying to find companionship and love? So what that the guy lived on a bike and had for years, and didn't seem to have a nickel to his name, and on closer questioning, didn't seem to know much about pediatric AIDS. None of this—nor Maddy's best efforts—was going to stop me.

When the day came for Bike Guy to leave town, I was sad. I had convinced myself he was my one and only. We decided we would stay in touch throughout his journey and try to meet along the way. And yes, I gave him a few hundred dollars to keep him afloat.

By lurking in the corner and listening to every word we uttered, Maddy became aware of this "loan." When he left, she accused me of paying to have a boyfriend. Where did she come by such cynicism? I was really starting to dislike my little wife, but because she was thirteen, a trial separation was out of the question.

When Bike Guy pulled out of the driveway on his bike, I was misty and playing out the drama for all it was worth. It turned out he had left a card behind with a note calling me his "angel." I was one smitten kitten, which made Maddy even angrier.

Over the course of the next few weeks, Bike Guy called regularly (from phone booths—collect), and each time I tried desperately to relate to his hunger and exhaustion. We arranged to meet in Regina, which is a mere fifteen hundred miles from Toronto. While I was making arrangements to fly out, Maddy stared at me, shaking her head, as if to say, *You should be so embarrassed*. Or worse, *You are a traitor*.

When I arrived in Regina, which is a small, extremely remote prairie town not exactly known for its culture, I was a bit cranky. I had had to get a connecting flight through Winnipeg, which was a pain in the ass. When I complained about this to Bike Guy, he looked at me as though I were the laziest, most spoiled creature on the planet. HE HAD RIDDEN HIS BIKE THERE and I'm bitching. We definitely inhabited different worlds—his, charitable and brave, and mine, selfish and materialistic. Not a recipe for a loving relationship.

We had an okay time in Regina, but I came home disappointed, and Maddy was only too happy to say, "I told you so." She was filled with such glee, I wanted to strangle her. More collect phone calls from Bike Guy followed, and unfortunately, a couple of the times I became demanding. I wanted some type of plan for our "relationship," which couldn't happen because he was living on a bike.

In the end, Bike Guy sent me a note—by fax—saying that he wasn't interested in me or my spoiled ways and that I was "introducing negative vibrations into his entourage." After hours of deciphering this sentence, Suzanne and I both concluded that he meant I was a "bummer" in his book. That hurt, but his broken English has become a mainstay in our library of humor, so I thank him for that. Of course, I wasn't going to take this dumping lying down, so I demanded that he pay me back the money I loaned him. He responded by calling me "a filthy capitalist." I hated to admit it, but Maddy had been right all along.

Bike Guy disappeared just as quickly as he had appeared, but he did send regular payments (in the form of one or two crumpled twenties) over the ensuing months and actually paid me back all my money.

When I look back now, it was ridiculous for me to think that a relationship with him could have ever worked. But, at the time, it didn't change the fact that I was living with a thirteen-year-old who was determined to sabotage any chance I had at a relationship.

She had made her intentions known, and she was quickly becoming the enemy.

CHAPTER 10

"DESPERADO"

Maddy

I never liked any of the men my mom dated. They were never good enough for her or for any decent woman, for that matter. What's worse, I felt as though I was the only one smart enough to see through all of their bullshit and that my mom was blinded by the prospect of love. She made the decision to be a single parent early in the game, so I made the decision that I would have to be her protector.

When I was six, I made her promise me that she would never marry again; when I was eight, I made her promise that she would never have any more children. Looking back now, I realize I wasn't willing to share her with anyone else—no matter how much candy or how many toys her boyfriends bought me. Though I hate to admit it, I had a knack for scaring her suitors away. I looked as sweet as could be, but I had started fine-tuning a temper. It was already hard for my mom to find guys that were willing to overlook the fact that she had two kids, but when one of those kids threw a temper tantrum, forget about it.

When I was thirteen, my tantrum-based, warding-off system was still a work in progress, until the day I met Bike Guy. Where my mother picked him up was beyond me. He sort of just appeared one day. He had shoulder-length dark hair that he wore in a ponytail, and he thought he was all that and a bag of chips. I hated him from the moment I met him. Why would anybody want to ride around the world on a bike? How is that contributing to society? He said that he was doing it for charity, but the only charity case I could see was him.

Shortly after appearing, he moved in with us. After all, up until then he had been living on a freaking bike.

He got quite comfortable quite quickly and walked around the place like he owned it. He helped himself to anything in the fridge and sat on the couch watching television while my mom worked. The whole idea, I had thought, was for my mom to find a fellow adult, not another mooch. Ian and I had that one covered. I had nothing to say to the guy—nothing nice, that is. We forced small talk. I don't know how he felt comfortable. Here was a woman allowing him to sleep at her house, eat her food, and laze about. She had a daughter who obviously hated him, and he was contributing nothing. This would bother an average man and make him feel like a failure, but not when he's a con artist!

I was thirteen and wanted nothing more than to be exactly like my friends, and none of my friends' parents were dating guys on world bike tours. I tried to play it off that he was just my mom's friend, but my friends knew that "friends" don't sleep in the same bed as my mother. I couldn't believe that she was doing this to me. I knew what sex was and found the whole concept disgusting. I also knew that when you're having sex with someone, they sleep in your bed. I didn't want any guy doing such a disgusting thing to her. I wondered why I had to be stuck with a mother like that.

I started off slowly with my tantrums, but all that got me was trouble (apparently I was too old). That's when I started trying to build allies. My first hit was Ian. He didn't like the guy either but was too busy being fifteen to care and didn't want to risk getting on Mom's bad side. I decided to go higher up the ladder to Kim, my mom's sister, but she wasn't committed to the war. She was hoping that Bike Guy would make my mom happy. That's when I decided to go straight to the top—to Nanna. If I could get her on my side, then I was sure to win. One day my Mom and I, with Bike Guy in tow of course, went to Nanna's apartment for a swim in her pool. This was my opportunity to align with Nanna, who surely could not like this Rico Suave look-alike.

I did it all. I gave him dirty looks, and whenever he said something dumb, I looked at Nanna, the matriarch, with a "See what I mean?" stare. That's when she told me to come for a swim with her.

"Maddy, doesn't your mom deserve to be happy?" she asked.

I couldn't believe what she was saying. Of course she deserved to be happy, but not with this jackass.

"He's a nice guy and likes your mom, and she obviously likes him, so cut it out. I know what you're doing," she said.

Had they all lost their minds? I was convinced he was nothing like the saint they took him for.

I got out of the pool angry that sunny afternoon and wondered where to go from there. Out of the corner of my eye I saw Bike Guy reach over and put his hand on my mom's leg. I wanted to scream at him to get his greasy hand off of her. I envisioned throwing the table over and lunging for his head so that I could rip out his Fabio ponytail. As I sat at the table looking at his stupid face, I did the only thing I had left: I cried.

Later in the week it came to my attention that Mr. Suave was getting ready to mount his bike and ride off into the sunset. I had almost forgotten about my number one ally: time. As Mick Jagger once said: Time was on my side. Before Bike Guy left, he had a couple of things to do, like use my mom's connections for publicity regarding his bike ride and borrow money from her. I, of course, overheard all of this. You would think that before deciding to ride around the world, he would have made some sort of financial plan, but no.

I hoped that we wouldn't hear from him again, but my mom thought that there was a chance for them somewhere down the road. He didn't keep in contact as far as I know. After that, my entire family confessed that they had disliked him from the get-go (whatever) and claimed to have always known he wasn't a keeper. I didn't argue the fact that I had known it all along, because, hey, I don't like to brag.

Shortly after Bike Guy rode out of her life, my mom asked

me why it was okay for my dad to be remarried and have someone, but it wasn't okay for her. I told her that I wanted her to be happy and to find love but that she simply had bad taste. I also couldn't understand why she needed a man. She wasn't alone. She had us.

In the years since, I often think back to the desperation with which she held on to the hope of falling in love, and at twenty-two, I now understand it.

But back then, what did I know?

I was just thirteen.

Chapter 11

Timber!

Joan

It was a fine Friday evening in May when I drove up to the woods to see my sister, Kim, and her husband, Mike, and to enjoy some beer and barbecue on their deck. As I was leaving the city, I experienced a rush of joy. The drive out was gorgeous—the grass was green, the flowers were blooming, and the sky was a perfect shade of pink. Life was good. Work was clicking along, and the kids weren't offering up any new forms of torture for me. In my euphoria, I decided I would buy Kim and Mike a new tree for their backyard—a random but lovely gesture, I thought as I drove toward them.

I got to their place and made the big announcement, and, as luck would have it, Kim had been thinking about getting a new tree too. So we spent the evening discussing different types of trees—of course, not knowing the first thing about them—and mapping out where to buy one. We put together a list of different tree farms in the area and fancied ourselves horticulturalists.

The next morning, despite having all the maps and locations of the farms and nurseries, we managed to get lost. As we traveled down a dirt road wondering where the hell we had gone wrong, lo and behold, there was a dingy sign that read TREES, pointing us toward a driveway. It wasn't the farm we were looking for, but we followed the sign and soon found another one that read YOU FOUND US. Bingo!

Instantly we spotted a tree that was going to fit the bill quite nicely. Just as we were oohing and aahing, a good-looking guy approached and asked if he could help us. *Well, yeah*, I thought. After about a half hour of discussing arborist issues (me pretending I knew quite a bit), we left with an order for a tree (for Kim and Mike's yard) and a promise that Tree Guy was going to come down to my place in Toronto to take a look at my backyard. Please understand that I had never, until that moment, considered doing anything with my garden, but man, I figured it was worth it just to check this guy out one more time.

When he came to the house, I instantly hired him to do some work in the yard. Standing in the kitchen looking out the window, Suzanne and I agreed that it was well worth the money if he took his shirt off while he was planting and pruning. Talking to him earlier while he worked, I had also ascertained that he was divorced, had two kids roughly the same ages as mine, and had a very good sense of humor. Things were looking up. He seemed like a kind, loving, tender man.

When Tree Guy started working on the place, Suzanne and I peeked through the curtains to stare at him as he worked. We were fortunate that it was about one hundred degrees those couple of days, and as luck would have it, as if he could read our minds, he took his shirt off. Of course, I was outside "consulting" with him about "tree stuff" as much as possible. I was also worried that he might get dehydrated in the heat, so I made sure I was there to serve him lots of water. Simply put, I was developing quite the crush.

Things were proceeding nicely with Tree Guy, but my house at the time was a three-ring circus. We were operating the entire Canadian Teletubbies empire out of my basement. The company in New York was leasing the house along with me, so it was a fancy basement, but nevertheless, chaotic. The upside was that "The Barbie Dream House," as we affectionately called it, made me look like I really had it going on. It was a very stately looking gray stucco house with marble counters, a couple of fireplaces, and a master suite. I thought I had died and gone to heaven.

The second day into Tree Guy's work, I had people coming in and out at various times throughout the day—everyone from our superslick apparel manufacturer to our incredibly down-to-earth public television children's broadcaster. At the end of the day, a couple of us decided it would be a great idea if we all sat down with some cocktails after a hard day's work, and what the hell, maybe we should invite Tree Guy. (This mission was ticking along according to plan, so far without a hitch.)

The stage was set and Tree Guy said, sure, he'd love to hang out once he got finished. This was as good as it got. The evening wasn't quite as dignified as I would have liked, or should I say I wasn't as dignified as I would have liked, thanks to a couple of drinks too many, what with the excitement of it all. Regardless, the next morning I had decided I was going to marry him.

During the evening's entertaining, I hadn't seen all that much of the kids. I got them dinner, but they were making themselves pretty scarce, which was so easy in "The Barbie Dream House." However, I was feeling some rather sinister vibes from Maddy. She was like a cat, kind of tucked up against a wall, watching me with a rather evil glint in her eye. Her behavior wasn't overt, but not that long ago Bike Guy had been on the scene. I instinctively knew I was going to have to keep an eye on this situation and remain in control.

Tree Guy promised to call me the next day as he headed out to his beat-up pickup truck. I thought, my God, I've bagged the Marlboro Man. This was excellent. He called the next day. No men in my life had ever called when they were supposed to, so I loved him for that alone. Apparently, getting my love didn't take much.

In the middle of all this elation and love was Maddy, the simmering, fifteen-year-old she-devil. She had not taken well to Tree Guy. He wasn't at the house much, but when he was, she would throw tantrums over absolutely nothing and spew such ugliness that tranquil Tree Guy was shocked. What I didn't realize was that Maddy was merely putting her plan into action—what better way to get her momma back into her loving arms than to drive away any shot at happiness with a third party? What I hadn't factored into this equation was that Tree Guy was doing some simmering of his own and growing more and more disdainful of Maddy's antics by the day. He hadn't shared this with me along the way, of course, as is so often the way with men. Why communicate?

I was feeling the love, so I did what any self-respecting idiot would do and invited Tree Guy to our summer cottage to share a couple of days of family vacation with not only Maddy and her friend, but also with Kim and Mike and their two preteen boys. I had only known the guy for three weeks—what was I thinking?

Tree Guy showed up at the cottage several hours late in his truck. I walked out to the driveway to greet him, and he climbed out dressed up as Thurston Howell, the guy on *Gilligan's Island* that dresses like a cheesy, rich yachtsman. I am not kidding—he had on the blazer with the crest, the captain's hat, and some type of god-awful pair of pants. He thought it was hilarious. I demanded that he change in his car and told him that there was no way he could enter the premises looking like that. Who goes to those lengths for such a stupid joke? Tree Guy did not take kindly to being told what to do. I saw something in his eyes that should have sent me running in the other direction. But instead, I got scared and awkward. I wanted to set things right so everything would run smoothly. Regardless, he would still have to shake the outfit.

After he changed out of his getup, I took Tree Guy down to the so-called beach. To get to the beach, we had to walk through soaking-wet grass, which I'm pretty sure was soaked with sewage. This cottage was proving to be one of our worst rentals yet. We had rented places with no heating, bad-crazy appliances, the odd bug, but none was as bad as this place. It was infested with earwigs, which was making our neurotic, urban brats crazy. And the beach sucked. All this for a mere two thousand dollars a week.

To make matters worse, Maddy had spent the morning dying her hair the most horrific shade of blond and insisted on keeping dark roots. Her boobs were spilling out of her tight tank top, and I'm pretty sure she and her friend Chris were stoned the entire time. At least, I told myself, she wasn't being belligerent.

When we got down to the beach, Maddy gave Tree Guy a look that said, *What the hell are you doing here?* Here we go again, I thought. Let the games begin.

We all hung out at the shitty beach for a little while but gave up when we decided we could definitely smell something resembling human waste. We weren't going to let it get us down, though. Instead, we all headed up to the cottage to play board games and drink some beer.

Within a couple of hours Tree Guy was teaching my nephews how to gamble with real money. This was not going over well at all with Kim, and she tried diplomatically to let Tree Guy know that she didn't think this was the best cottage activity for a couple of young boys.

Maddy was doing everything she could to alienate Tree Guy. And if she had to piss him off and offend him to get him out of there, that's what she would do. She was, after all, defending home and hearth. Once we finally got dinner on the table, Maddy sat down and announced that she and Chris were going into town that night to "drop some acid." Maddy, as far as I knew, had never done any hard drugs in her life, and furthermore, I was convinced that if she were indulging, she wouldn't be letting me in on the secret. Her charade was strictly for the benefit of Tree Guy, who looked like he wanted to reach across the table and strangle her. She had changed into another skintight tank top and had her new blond tresses down around her bare shoulders. A proud parental moment indeed.

I grabbed Maddy by the arm and took her into my bedroom and whisper/screamed (in the way only a frantic mother can) at her to pull it together, or I was going to send her home on the next bus. Well, in past years that would have been perceived as an unspeakable punishment, but not this year. She answered back in her own whisper/scream that that would be fine with her since she did not want any part of this "bullshit family vacation."

I hated her.

We managed to get through the evening in spite of the fact that both Kim and Maddy were developing a real full-on hatred for Tree Guy. To top it off, it was pouring rain, but we soldiered on.

The next morning things got worse. The continued downpour was now torrential, and before most of us had gotten up, Tree Guy was back at the crap table with the boys. Kim looked at me as though we weren't related. I honestly couldn't blame her since I happen to agree that gambling is probably not the best skill to pass along to a ten- and twelve-year-old pair of already rowdy boys. I gently suggested to Tree Guy that maybe Scrabble or Monopoly might be more fun. He looked at me like I was a complete idiot.

By the end of the day I was ready to blow the whole place up and everyone in it. Nobody was happy except Maddy. Tree Guy and I were barely speaking, Kim wanted to kill him, and the kids were wound up like tops thanks to a healthy dose of cabin fever and a newfound addiction to gambling.

I finally took Tree Guy outside and said he might want to respect Kim and Mike's wishes and back-burner the gambling, and he turned on me with pure venom. For starters, he kindly pointed out that my daughter was a complete asshole who was much more of a corrupting influence on her cousins than he ever could be. He also let me know that it was clear to him that I was a complete failure as a mother and was raising the daughter of Satan.

Okeydoke then.

How much could he possibly know about kids when his kids lived with their mother and visited him only every couple of weeks. I told him to piss off, pack up his Thurston Howell attire, and scram. Given the tight quarters, this was all done in my best whisper/scream.

As he drove down the driveway, leaving me in the dust, I stood like a zombie, my fists clenched at my sides. One word raced through my mind: *enough*. Enough with these men. Enough with this struggle—with trying and hoping and weaving and bobbing. Enough with Maddy and her snide remarks and know-it-all adolescent attitude. I was drowning in a pond of human waste. Enough was enough.

When I walked back into the cottage, the whole gang was awaiting my return. The sun had come out, and a calm had descended upon the place. But I still didn't want to be there. Never had I felt so tired and alone.

Chapter 12

Acid Trip

Maddy

Every summer since I was a child, my mom has rented a cottage. Northern Ontario in the summertime is beautiful. The days are hot and the lakes are the perfect antidote. But after spending fifteen summers there, I had gotten my fill of the cottage and hated the place. I had also decided that my mom was completely incapable of knowing what was right for me or for her. She had hooked up with a new boyfriend, and he was the worst one yet. She had hired him to landscape our property and invited him in for a drink at the end of a day's work. From then on I had a new enemy who would prove to be my biggest challenge. He waltzed into my house, dirty from working, and parked himself quite comfortably on the couch. I let him know that the war was on. I was borderline rude to him and snickered at his lame jokes. Tree Guy bothered me to no end. I couldn't find one thing about him that I liked. He mumbled when he talked, he dressed like an idiot from the eighties—think Don Johnson from *Miami Vice*—he was not funny, and the worst part of all, my mom actually liked him.

I did everything to break them up, but nothing was working. I threw tantrums, which at the age of fifteen, I realize now, is just plain embarrassing. When the summer rolled around, I prayed that stupid Tree Guy wouldn't come to the cottage. The cottage that my mom rented seemed really nice when we got there. It had many rooms and a big-screen television in the finished basement. My girlfriend Chris and I called dibs on a room that was located in the basement with a cozy-looking queen-size bed. We took it easy that night and snuck out in the rain to smoke a joint. We decided to turn in at about midnight. Then we got into our pajamas, tucked ourselves into bed, and turned off the light. After talking for a couple of minutes, I told Chris to turn on the light because I felt like something was not right. That's when I saw hundreds of earwigs crawling all over the walls and ceiling. I ran upstairs where my mom was sitting with Aunt Kim and told them that there was no way in hell I would sleep down there. My mom didn't provide any solution and simply told us to put out bug traps and deal with our new roommates until the weekend was over.

When my mom warned me about acting up when Tree Guy got there, I looked at her like I was insulted by her even suggesting that I would misbehave. I hoped one of his trees would fall on his head causing amnesia, leaving him unaware of who my mom was and ending their ridiculous relationship.

But he came up as planned. Chris and I spent our time figuring out where we could go to smoke our joints secretly. For the first time in years, it rained almost every day. I, of course, viewed this as Tree Guy's fault. "He brought this weather with him. He's always getting in the way of my good time," I told Chris. She looked at me like I had lost my mind. She tried to keep me separated from him. At dinner I would sit across from him, staring daggers in his direction and scoffing at his stupid jokes. One night Chris and I had caught wind that there was a dance in town and saw this as a good opportunity to make some friends. My mom agreed to take us, since for her it would mean a couple of tension-free hours.

Chris and I walked through the town and discovered that there was nothing going on, so we smoked a joint by the marina. Thankfully, there was an open convenience store nearby, so we hit it up for some much-needed munchies. We managed to meet the only black guy in the whole town and decided that he would be our new friend. He was gorgeous. He had a wild fro like Sideshow Bob from *The Simpsons*. We all got to talking and he invited us to his house, where we hung out until our curfew, then took a cab home.

The next day was actually partially sunny, and Chris and I thought that a change to my look was in order. Months before, I had chopped off all my long hair and now wanted to improve on the dramatic change. Chris and I bought a box of bleach and got to work on the dock outside the cabin. Truth be told, we should have read the instructions a little more carefully. After I dried my hair, I looked in the mirror. The roots were practically white, the middle was an awful blond, and the ends were a weird shade of muted orange. I convinced myself that it didn't look that bad. Chris and I laughed, but when my mom saw me, she shook her head with disgust and walked away. She didn't want to yell at me in front of Tree Guy. That night at dinner I told my mom that I wanted to go into town, and when she said no, I flipped out. I got mad and told her I wanted to go into town to do acid. I wasn't really going to *do* acid, but I guess she didn't see the humor in the comment. I think the fact that I said it in front of my little cousins and her new boyfriend was what really pissed her off. She took me into the other room and started yelling. I took it for all of thirty seconds before I started yelling back. She told me to stay in the room, but as soon as she left, I stormed out.

Everyone was looking at me like I had lost it. Not only had I crossed the line, but now I was also completely disregarding my mom's punishment for my already bad behavior. I screamed at her, and then I turned to Tree Guy and told him off. I told him that I hated him and even went so far as to call him an idiot, which, when said properly, is very harsh and effective. Meanwhile everyone was sitting at the table in stunned silence. I told Chris to get up and that we were going into town whether we had my mom's blessing or not. The poor girl sat there not knowing what to do. Carefully, she looked at my mom, put her head down, and stood up. My mom told me that if I walked out the door, I wouldn't be welcomed back. I grabbed my bag and headed out the door.

My mom threw up her hands and told my aunt to give us

a ride to town. In my head I had won the battle, but in reality I knew my mom just wanted me out. When Chris and I got back that night, Tree Guy was still there. I sat at the table and glared at him. He slammed his hands down on the table and stormed out.

He left the next day.

I guess he was sick and tired of dealing with me.

Driving home after our week's vacation, I sat in the back of the car, allowing Ian dibs on the front seat, and stared at the back of my mom's head. Maybe I should have dropped that acid? Maybe I shouldn't have dyed my hair? What did it matter anyway? I was so over this place.

CHAPTER 13

SWEET SIXTEEN

Joan

Maddy was the delightful age of sixteen, but there was nothing sweet about her. I had been promoted to president of the entertainment divisions at my fancy company—in other words, I had hit pay dirt. I didn't think it was a big deal until everyone kept congratulating me on my "rise up the corporate ladder." I could never have imagined that I would be living the lifestyle I was at the ripe old age of forty-one. The only glitch was that I was never home—my boss owned me, heart and soul, and knew how to play me like a banjo. He had an amazing ability to prey on my fear and guilt (which are two of the biggies for me). I did whatever he wanted and that included flying to New York on an hour's notice and talking to him on the phone every day, ten hours a day, day or night (even when we weren't together on business trips).

In spite of it all, I was learning how to do business and was actually making enough money to get out of debt, get a new car (that alone was a huge financial feat), and buy a house. Getting fat and letting the household slip into the abyss seemed like a small price to pay for financial security for the kids and myself. As a matter of fact, the money that I made and saved during my four and a half years at that job makes the life I have today possible. Sometimes we just have to hand over the controls and let go. Thanks to all of my business travel, part of me was relieved that I was at least missing SOME of the outrageous "stunts" the kids were pulling at that point. I was only kidding myself though, because somehow they always made me aware of whatever it was that was going on. They say now that they hid a ton of stuff from me and lied like crazy, but it sure felt like I was privy to way more than my friends were with their kids. I have always cursed the day that I decided communication was important with the kids. Ignorance can be bliss.

Over the years, I have prided myself on the fact that the kids have always shown a healthy respect for my stuff. They were never allowed to go into my purse without asking. Of course, to make sure, I slept with my purse beside my bed for years. Maddy would occasionally go into my closet and help herself to clothing, which pissed me off to no end. But for the most part, what was mine was mine, and they respected that.

One night I was in London in my hotel room with my limo driver, a guy with a great sense of humor whom I had befriended. We were having a couple of drinks after a rough day. I had started the day in Paris, where I had to sit down with fifteen irate French executives who all thought I was just another filthy North American. They accused me at various points during the meeting of being unprofessional and someone they would never do business with again. That was fine by me, since the contract we were living with at that point was something that was signed before I had come on board. These people had gotten my bosses to agree to the most ridiculous terms, so we were trying to rectify the situation. I did not care what they thought of me, but I was pretty burned out by the time I left their office. I was traveling with one of our employees based in Germany, and she and I were not getting along so well. And I had quit smoking for the first time. I bitched about everything from the hotel accommodation to the food. After a couple of years of this insane travel schedule, I was exhausted.

As karma would have it, I left my suitcase in the back of a cab in Paris later in the day, just before going to the airport to catch a flight to London. I freaked out and unfairly blamed my associate. I am ashamed of some of my behavior during that time. I was becoming accustomed to being treated like a queen. I had a driver when I was in London, for God's sake—who did I think I was? Without my luggage, I had no clothes or toiletries but still had to catch my flight in order to make my meetings in London the following morning. I found a crummy store that sold I LOVE THE UK T-shirts and Diana china, where I bought a sweat suit and a pair of awful running shoes, a delightful ensemble that made me look like Austin Powers. I also grabbed some ugly underwear and socks. I had enough stuff to get by until my flight home later the next day, and I still hadn't smoked. *Everything is going to be fine*, I told myself.

Just as I was relaxing (of course, looking like a complete jackass) with previously mentioned limo driver, the phone rang. It was Maddy sobbing uncontrollably from Toronto. I thought she was possessed. It was worse. It turns out, she had, without a driver's license or lessons (she was just too lazy), taken my brand-new company car (a BMW X5) out for a drive the night before. She was upset because she was stopped by the police and they took it away. When I screamed into the phone to ask why the fuck she would do that, she explained that her girlfriend was really drunk and had no way to get home. I can't even get started on how much is wrong with that statement, but what was I going to do? I was in London in my Princess Diana suite with my driver. Fortunately, I was going to be home the next day and would be able to pick up the car at the pound on my way home from the airport, and it would cost "only" two hundred dollars. Maddy seemed to understand how bad it was. She admitted that she had never been so irresponsible (or so I naively thought). I concluded this was just one of those ridiculous lapses in judgment we all have. I couldn't let it get to me or I would light up a cigarette. Keep it together, I told myself; everything is going to be okay.

The next morning, Maddy was on the phone again, still hysterical, which I thought was a good sign. She swore she would never do anything like that again and I explained as calmly as I could that she would be paying the $120 ticket and the $200 car pound fee. She swore up and down she would get some babysitting jobs and put every dime she could toward the costs. During that expensive overseas phone call, I told her to stop worrying and that I hoped she had learned a valuable lesson.

I landed in Toronto at 1:00 a.m. the following day—which put me at six in the morning, Western European Time. Fortunately, I was flying business class thanks to my gazillion travel points. I grabbed a cab and headed straight for the car pound, where the guys had a good laugh about my spoiled brat taking my BMW for a spin. Then I headed home. Maddy had told me that she would be staying at her dad's that night, which was confirmed by him, so at least I could get some sleep. I was getting angrier at the situation as the hours went by, so I wasn't quite ready to face her.

By 1:00 p.m. the next day she still hadn't surfaced, so I called her dad and was told that no, she hadn't been there last night. I discovered during this conversation that she had not been there most of the week I had been gone. What the hell had been going on? It boiled down to this: It was spring break and she had, at the age of sixteen, been freewheeling around town for days with little or no supervision. Each time I had spoken to her during the week, she had assured me that everything was fine and that she was staying at her dad's—which had been confirmed along the way by him. So what the hell happened? He explained calmly that he had been in close touch with her, but she had just stayed at her girlfriends' a few times. I slammed down the phone and decided my battle was with her, not him.

In the meantime, I got a collect call from Ian, who was in Acapulco. He was enjoying spring break with his class in Mexico; it was his last year of high school. He sounded like he was having the time of his life so I tried to be friendly until he informed me that he had pierced his ear and gotten a tattoo. Whoa. I went nuts—I hated tattoos and had always made it clear that the kids were welcome to them only once they were living on their own and paying their own bills. Ian didn't know what was going on at home with his baby sister, so hadn't realized that I was on the verge of a psychopathic episode. He quickly explained that the tattoo was just henna, which was temporary. I told him what was going on and that I was very happy he was having a good time but too much detail was not going to work for me right at that moment. We got off the phone with the usual "I love you's," and I returned my focus to the missing person I wanted to kill.

After calling around to her various buddies, I finally found Maddy at her girlfriend's and demanded she get her butt home immediately. She *still* didn't come home right away. She wanted to have coffee and a bit of breakfast first. I was getting crazier and crazier as the time crawled by, so when the little car thief finally walked in the door, I was completely out of control. I greeted her with a slap across the face—something I am not particularly proud of, but she had this belligerent look on her face that just sent me over the edge. She looked at me as though I was a complete monster that should be put away for a very long time. She screamed in my face and told me that she was going to call Child Services. I handed over the phone and suggested that she might enjoy a life of foster homes. I pointed out that "children" don't drive cars, which seemed to take the wind out of her sails—but not for long.

The screaming started up again when I told her she was grounded for a month without allowance. She turned on me like the feral cat she had become and told me I had no right to tell her what to do. I explained to her that that statement could not be more misguided. Did she understand that stealing the car was a big deal? As was drinking underage? Not to mention acting like a free and easy bachelorette all week?

How had she gone from the crying little baby on the phone when I was in England to this cold, hateful little creature? I informed her that she was going to have to place a call to my boss to apologize. She didn't see that one coming at all. He had treated her very well over the few years I had been working for him. She looked up to him. She couldn't understand why on earth she would have to make that call. I simply stated that he had paid for the car. When she reluctantly made the call, he explained to her in his coldest tone that she could have caused a lot of trouble for the company and me. After all, we were a children's entertainment company and her mother was the president. God help us all if the press got a hold of this. In reality, the press wouldn't have given a damn, but she didn't know that. She apologized to my boss and told him she had no idea that her joyride could have resulted in the destruction of his empire. He didn't let up, and when he hung up on her, she was white. Always handy to have a hard-ass in your corner.

Kim drove down later that day for a visit. Maddy came

downstairs (I had sent her to her room) about fifteen times to beg, cajole, and scream for release so that she could go to her friend's sweet sixteen. Honestly, whoever came up with the idea that a sixteen-year-old girl is sweet has never had one. She didn't let up for about three hours. When it finally became clear to her that she was not getting a release, she slammed her bedroom door and was mercifully quiet for the rest of the night.

I was running on empty—in the space of twenty-four hours I had flown across the Atlantic, picked up my car at the car pound, slapped my daughter in the face, and learned that my son had pierced his ear in Mexico.

I swear, I didn't think I was going to make it. Little did I know, things were about to get worse. Much worse.

CHAPTER 14

IN THE DRIVER'S SEAT

Maddy

I really hit my stride at sixteen. I was independent in the sense that my mom wasn't around to see what I was doing, and when she was there, I laid a guilt trip on so thick that she turned a blind eye to me. Anytime I was punished, I knew that it would come to a swift end the second that she packed her bag to go on another business trip. My whole philosophy was, it's easier to ask for forgiveness than permission. And it seemed to be working for me.

I wasn't going to school. I was already going to fail at least one class if not more, so I made it my number-one priority to have as much fun as possible and did whatever I wanted, whenever I wanted.

I was an idiot. I was skipping school in the name of self-education and smoking a lot of weed. I thought that society's rules were made to prevent everybody from having fun. Police were just there to bust our parties.

Spring break was always a great time for us, a week to unwind from our stressful, teenage lives. My mother and brother were going to be out of the country, which meant that all of the parties could come to me and I wouldn't have to leave my house in the cold weather. I was supposed to be staying with my dad, and each night I told him that I would be sleeping at some friend's house. Instead, I created a nice bachelorette pad at my mom's house. One particular night, my friend Chris and I were hanging out when one of the coolest guys invited us to a party at his house. We had to go in style. The solution came to us at the same time. We could take my mom's new BMW X5. The only problem was that neither one of us had a license or even a learner's permit.

The previous summer we had gone to our friend's cottage with her grandfather and run into a similar predicament. We desperately needed to get into town but the walk was just too far, so we told the old man that I had my license. He let us borrow his boat of a car and waved us good-bye. I was nervous because I had never driven, but pulled through beautifully. Driving on the highway was exciting, and we got to town safe and sound to do our very important errands. We bought a case of beer and Lotto tickets and made it back to the cottage in one piece. So when Chris and I were trying to decide whether to take my mom's car, whether I had experience was obviously not an issue.

We sat for about half an hour, kicking the idea around. We

then made a pro and con list. On the pro side we had a lot of legitimate arguments, like looking cool, saving money on cabs, listening to good music, and, well, looking cool came up twice. On the con side we could come up with only one argument— getting caught. Failing my learner's permit test only weeks prior should have probably been put that on that list too.

Right after the list was done, our friend called saying that if we didn't pick her up, she couldn't go. It was decided. We had to take the car. The fact that after forty-five minutes of debating we reasoned that breaking the law was necessary proves not only my idiocy but also the idiocy of my friends. We found a map and figured out how to get all over the city by taking just side streets, which, in our heads, guaranteed not getting caught.

Next we needed to find the keys. I knew that my mom often hid them when out of town to ensure that Ian wouldn't take her car, but she would never suspect me. I called her in England and told her that I had forgotten a CD in her car and that I needed to know where the keys were. She told me, oblivious to the trouble that I was planning. If I had put into school half of the energy I spent planning schemes, I would have been a straight-A student.

I jumped behind the wheel. Chris stood at the end of my driveway looking for oncoming traffic and waved me on. We laughed with pure glee as we started our journey. Driving the deserted side streets was fine, but when it came to major intersections, I was unclear as to the actual rules of the road. Was I able to turn left on a green? I didn't know and neither did my copilot, so we just held our breath and went for it. After picking our friend up at one end of the city, we departed for the other end. We were getting close to the party when my friend complimented me on my driving skills. I was feeling like a million bucks. The driveway to the house party was more of a challenge than it looked. We had called people to come out and meet us so that they could see how really cool we were. We started into the drive when the snow bank on the left came out of nowhere. The whole car went on a tilt, almost tipping over. We all screamed and slowly backed up. So much for our great entrance. It took me three tries until I finally parked.

The party was lame. I realized I hadn't thought this through when I remembered that people weren't allowed to drink and drive. Definitely a point for the con side that we had overlooked. We left the party shortly after arriving and went over to a girlfriend's house. That was boring too, so we decided to drop this guy off at the other end of the city. After we dropped him off, the plan was to go back to my house and drink. We would get some gas and then head straight home. Since by this time I was superexperienced, we didn't see a need for the side streets and decided to go straight down Eglington, one of Toronto's main streets. About five minutes into our drive home, and in the middle of a great song, we passed a police cruiser. Thinking nothing of it, we kept bobbing to our beats. When the cops started following us, I chalked it up to nothing. When they turned on their sirens I thought maybe there was an emergency, but when they did the little *beep, beep*, I knew they wanted me. I considered making a run for it, but I didn't know if that meant having to change to four-wheel drive or something. I pulled over and immediately started shaking. I looked at Chris, panic-stricken. She didn't look much better.

I rolled down my window as the cops walked up to the car. "What seems to be the problem, Officer?" I had heard that line spoken in countless movies. One of the officers explained to me that my rear light wasn't on, which meant that my main lights weren't on either. I had no idea that you had to physically turn them on. I assumed that it would happen automatically when you turned the key. I mean, the car *was* an automatic. He asked me for my license, which I told him I had left at home. He asked me for my personal information, which I also lied about. I didn't lie about my name, just about my age. I made myself a year older so that I would be at the right age to have an actual license. The officer went back to his car, while the other officer continued talking to poor Chris. I thought that I had tricked them and had gotten off with only a ticket for not having my lights on. I asked the female officer talking to Chris how much a ticket would run me. When she told me twenty-five dollars, I thought that this was my lucky day. I was practically chuckling with the female officer, making jokes about how much of a scatterbrain I was. When the male officer came back to my window, I extended my hand to take my ticket, smiling at how silly the whole thing was. He told me to turn off the car, which I thought was kind of odd, but then again, what did I know? He looked me square in the eyes and said, "You don't have your license, do you?"

My smile vanished; my mind raced for the correct answer

when I remembered to deny, deny, deny. "Yes, I do," I said, barely convincing myself.

"No, you don't."

I yelled, "YES, I DO." Yelling always makes a lie more believable, as though you're so insulted at the lack of trust that you have to defend yourself by getting loud and mad.

He then leaned in real close and said softly, "Listen, I know you don't have your license. I looked you up, so you'd better admit to it now, or you will be in even more trouble than you already are."

The sobbing had already begun when I officially admitted to not having my license. He even reminded me that I had failed my learner's permit.

I got out of the car when the tow truck arrived to take it to the impound lot where it would stay until my mom could pick it up. I was still crying but had also become angry when the male officer said, "Do you know how lucky you are that we aren't arresting you right now?"

I replied in a broken voice, "Not that lucky. I got caught."

As we watched them tow my mother's BMW away, I saw, in that car, my freedom being towed away right along with it. Then a carful of teenagers not unlike us (although probably licensed) drove by and laughed. By this time I was hyperventilating and had huge puffy eyes and snot all over my face. The night had not gone as planned. We weren't cool. Our pro list was blown to shit. The cops even gave me the honor of telling my mom at my leisure. I would have rather they told her, so I wouldn't have had to weather her initial shock.

I had three days until she got back from England. After trying everything to get that car back, I needed to face the music. I had already told my dad what I had done in hopes that he could get the car, but he told me he couldn't as he was not married to my mom and had no right to get her car out of the pound. I called my mom while at a friend's house and told her, "I did something bad." She asked what it was I had done. I told her that I had taken out her new car and that it had been impounded. All she asked was what I had done to the car. I assured her that the car was in perfect condition. She told me to go to my dad's house, which I still hadn't been to, and that she would deal with me later. When I got to my dad's place, he tried to give me a lecture, and I ran away. I hid in an alley with Chris and watched my dad drive by looking for me. I felt kind of bad, but I knew I would feel worse listening to why I was such an idiot.

My mom arrived the next day. Facing her was like facing an executioner. She asked why I took the car in the first place, which is when I went right into my excuse. I simply had to save the day by driving my drunk friend because no one had any money for a cab and the only alternative was her driving herself. Naturally, I couldn't drive her car because there was no money for me to take a cab from her house. It was a mouthful, but I got it all out in one turn. I thought it was a great tale of me doing the responsible thing. She didn't buy it.

The next day I received more phone calls than I ever had in one day, even on a birthday, from disappointed relatives and family friends. The lectures didn't bother me since I could sit in my room, put the phone away from my ear, and secretly roll my eyes. Every now and then I would chime in with a "yeah" or "I know." At one point my mom decided that I needed to call her boss and apologize to him. I reluctantly agreed. When he answered the phone, his voice sounded distant and professional, as though I hadn't had a close relationship with him. He told me that since the car was half the company's, my escapade reflected badly on the company, which made things worse than I had ever thought. He took it a step further, saying, "The press would have a field day if this came out, maybe causing the collapse of the entire company." As a result of me being so egotistical, I believed that I had this power. I wasn't so selfish as to not have this upset me, however. I didn't want hundreds of unemployed people hating me because it was my fault they didn't have a job. He ended the conversation with, "I can no longer have a relationship with you. It's bad for the company's image."

I was mortified. How could he put all of this on me, for God's sake? I was *only* sixteen. Of course, the irony didn't escape me. The day before, I was using my age of sixteen to prove that I was almost an adult and could make my own decisions.

That night while I was trying to fall asleep, I sorted out a few things in my head, like, what would I wear while being chased down the street by paparazzi and what would the headlines be?

The next morning I woke with an awful feeling in my stomach, like something wasn't right. I can't describe what it was. I should have felt victorious.

But instead I just felt little and alone.

CHAPTER 15

MOTHER'S DAY!

Joan

In 2000, my fancy-pants job went down the tubes after my parent company decided my Canadian subsidiary was no longer viable. No longer was I going to be a highfalutin executive for a big, successful U.S. company—life as I had known it for a few years was about to change.

I decided to set up a new business with my assistant, Suzanne. Don't get me wrong: I wasn't starting my own company because I possessed any kind of burning entrepreneurial passion or drive. As always, I just had to pay the bills. The new company was going to allow some good things from the old life to remain the same—Suzanne and I could still be together and have the same kind of freedom and flexibility that we had gotten used to while working for a company in another country. We could be late for work, we could still shop at Old Navy whenever we felt like it for the bargains and elastic-waist pants, and we could stay in town. No one would be looking over our shoulder.

So we started our own company with some pretty realistic expectations, or so we thought. It was anything but easy. I had to throw my savings into it and put up with some of the biggest sharks around. Fiscal restraint became a part of our household reality, something that hadn't been a factor when I was with my old company. The kids were cool about it, but only when they didn't want something. The days of fancy business trips were no more. I was okay with it since the "big spender" role never really fit me, and I was able to sleep in my own bed for more than three nights in a row.

Maddy was not doing very well at school. She was crawling her way through grade twelve. Between her low confidence, lack of interest, crazy social life, and, well, sheer laziness, it was getting harder and harder to get her to focus on academics. I was doing my best, and everybody kept telling me that's all I could do.

Surprisingly—or not so surprisingly, at this point—Maddy began getting involved on the political front. Maddy's "activist ways" had been heating up for a few years. It started when she first appeared in the newspaper, being interviewed in grade eight about the "fascists" that ran her school. The school board had imposed a new rule forbidding girls from wearing tank tops to school. Well, my God, the righteous indignation that sprang from that was quite something. Maddy had a fire in her belly. The board's action was outrageous and there was no damn way she was going to take it lying down. First she started a petition. She roamed the halls of the school getting as many signatures as she could and had a series of meetings with the principal. When all that failed, she did what any self-respecting activist would and turned to the media. They printed an interview in our local newspaper with her speaking out about the injustice that was being inflicted on the young women of her generation. She didn't win that one, at least not right away, but it didn't stop her from focusing her activist energies on other "burning" issues. When she was eighteen, she decided to march for peace and supported the Canadian government's decision to stay out of the Iraq war. She loved Jean Chrétien, our prime minister, for trying to pass legislation for gay marriage and, more important, for the legalization of marijuana. What wasn't to love about such a leader?

When she was seventeen, she attended a pro-marijuana march in Toronto. I'll never forget how she came home afterward, mighty hungry and fired up on her activist experience. Her food intake was astounding. I had been having one of those rare June Cleaver days and cooked up what I thought was a ton of souvlakis on the barbecue. I also had made a delicious salad and, really lucky for her, cookies. I thought that she had worked up an appetite out in the heat during the march and went along with her extreme consumption of food. It was only when Ian gave me a face like "look at her" and started laughing that I realized she had the munchies. Duh—how stupid was I getting in my middle years?

In between bites she went on and on about how pot was

way safer than alcohol. She explained in her most earnest way that you never hear of a fight breaking out as a result of someone smoking a joint and no way was it addictive. I half listened with the phony interest that every mother knows well and served her more food.

The following year she fancied herself a veteran. She had felt at home the previous year at the march and loved all the people she had met. The girls, a.k.a. her posse, had had a great day and decided to do it again. This time they were photographed by the national newspaper. When she came home and told me this, I stopped dead in my tracks and wheeled on her, screaming, "What on God's earth were you doing in the photographs?" She was surprised at my alarm and quickly doused the fire by telling me that they were harmless photos and that she was just hanging out, having a laugh. I didn't believe that the photographer was just interested in some sweet portraits of teenage girls enjoying harmless fun, but her word was good enough for me—at least for the time being.

A couple of weeks passed and no photo of Maddy or her friends appeared in the newspaper. I wasn't overly worried about it, just relieved I had dodged another bullet. It was spring, the new company was looking promising, and the house was great (the first one I had owned in a while), so I wasn't going to let her activism bust my newfound Zen attitude.

When I was growing up, Mother's Day was a huge day for our family, especially since my mom was raising four of us by herself. My mom made damn sure none of us ever forgot to get her a card and some small token of our eternal gratitude for the kindness she showed us every other day of the year. We made her breakfast in bed and put together a decent dinner. We washed the dishes and made sure she spent that one day each year doing nothing. Or at least that's how I remember it.

I, on the other hand, had been screaming at my kids every Mother's Day for years to show some appreciation. For the past several years I'd been doing well if I got a homemade card. Now, some of you might think a homemade card is sweet, but from where I sit, if the teens in question are rich enough to be clubbing and wearing designer togs paid for by their starving, single mother, then a real card and a few flowers shouldn't be too much to ask. Sure, when they were little and still jumping out of bed at the crack of dawn, I would get breakfast in bed, but as the darlings got older and more nocturnal, the breakfast went by the wayside.

Ian has come through a couple of times when he's had a bit of cash, but dear Maddy . . . nothing. Don't get me wrong, her homemade cards are amazing and the sentiment expressed is always beautiful, but just once a trinket or something would have been nice. Anything that required her entering a store on my behalf would have been great.

The Mother's Day that Maddy was eighteen, however, took the cake in a way that none of us saw coming. My family and I had started a grand tradition of having our whole clan and any other stragglers over to my place for a big feast, some drinks, and of course, an exchange of flowers. My mom gave each of the women in the family (with kids) a single rose and a lovely card. Kim and I busted out our hostessing skills, cooking, cleaning, and screaming at all of our kids to just, for the love of God, leave us alone for a few hours. But it had turned into quite the extravaganza and was starting to wear on our nerves. It was time to switch it up. One evening, after a couple of drinks and a long afternoon of eating and chatting about the upcoming Mother's Day, the ladies in my family decided that we would all go to a restaurant for brunch. That way none of us would have to do anything but show up. The perfect plan!

It had been a few weeks since Maddy's marijuana march, so I believed the paper had scrapped any ideas of publishing Maddy's mug on their pages. The morning of Mother's Day started out like any other weekend morning—the kids asleep and me out running in the neighborhood. My new jogging passion was giving me the oomph I needed to stay off cigarettes, which I had abstained from for several months now. I was on fire and life was turning out not so bad.

When I got home, Maddy was heading to her new part-time job at a hot spot in the trendy area of Yorkville in Toronto. I was still shocked that she had been holding down this job for a few months and was beside myself with pride. On her way out the door, she mentioned that she was in the morning paper.

Uh-oh.

Why Mother's Day of all days? Was this someone's idea of a joke? I grabbed the paper out of her hand as she made a quick escape, promising to meet the family later for our prearranged Mother's Day brunch. I sat at the kitchen table and opened the paper. The photo wasn't just a thumbnail. It was a half page. Maddy was in the forefront in profile, with a record-breaking amount of smoke streaming out of her mouth. A couple of other girls lurked in the background, but there was no mistaking Maddy as the featured smoker. I can still imagine the photographer in the darkroom saying to one of his buddies, "Wouldn't it be funny to run this on Mother's Day?" Now, please note that there isn't one member of my family that doesn't have this particular paper delivered to their home every day. To make matters worse, it was in the front section—you know, with the hard news of the day.

I called Maddy on her cell phone asking her what on God's earth was I supposed to say to the family members we would be seeing in a few hours? She insisted that I just keep quiet and that there was a very good chance that no one would see the photo. Yeah, right. We have zero secrets in our family, which has been both a blessing and a curse over the years.

I was trying really hard not to lose it completely when Ian surfaced from the basement (a.k.a. his "lair") and took one look at the photo.

"Idiot."

Big help.

I called Kim. After she stopped laughing, she told me that I might as well bring the damn photo with me to the brunch and stare down my demons. Funny, but that wasn't what I wanted to hear.

Later that day after Ian shocked me with a card and some flowers and a kiss on the cheek, we drove to the restaurant. The whole time, Ian was shaking his head with disgust at his sister's ridiculousness.

When we sat down at the table, everybody was in a pretty good mood. My three nephews; my brother Bob and his wife, Pilar; Ian; Kim and Mike; and my mom were all there. I decided there was no time like the present, and I pulled the newspaper out of my bag and passed it quietly to my brother. I didn't think any of my siblings or their spouses would want this out in the open in front of their adolescent boys. My brother's face was the best. He just shook his head and looked at me with his winning smirk and asked, "How did she get so much smoke in her mouth?" He then handed my mother the evidence. She stared at it for a minute and then looked at me with the same smirk as Bob and asked, "How did she get that much smoke in her mouth?" I love my family for that—same thoughts, same reactions—and in this case the same appreciation for the ridiculous.

It was coming time for Maddy, the guest of honor, to show up, and we all joked that we might want to be prepared for a gang of paparazzi following close behind. She had always wanted fame, and now she was getting it. Having left her shift at the restaurant early, she came in looking absolutely gorgeous and fresh as a daisy—kind of like a movie star. The jabs started with my mother asking her about the amount of smoke she was exhaling and pushing her to tell us her secret. My mom has this way of really needling you, and in spite of her friendly demeanor, you know that you are getting nailed to the wall. My brother also prodded her about the quantity of smoke and asked in his friendliest tone if she was pleased with the composition of the shot. Kim and Mike ridiculed her pretty hard too. I remained silent. I'm sure she would have preferred to be screamed at than be subjected to this Irish form of torture. The ribbing lasted the entire meal and I never said a word.

Needless to say, Maddy hasn't been photographed in print since, for which I and the rest of the family are quite grateful. I think staring down the table at that bunch of senior smart-asses was enough to drive her underground.

CHAPTER 16

HELPING HANDS

Maddy

Being an activist has always been in my makeup. When I was young, it took the form of screaming until I got my way. At five, I think I liked standing up for what I believed in because it was a form of rebellion. As I got older, I turned my rebellious nature to fixing society. This started in grade eight when the school board decided that girls wearing tank tops was inappropriate, as it could distract the boys. They ruled that no shirt that revealed a girl's bra strap would be allowed. If this rule was not obeyed, the girl in question would be sent directly home to change and not allowed back until she had. It didn't seem fair. The boys were wearing their pants around their ankles (this was not a distraction for the girls, however, as the boys looked like idiots, but that's neither here nor there). All I wanted was equality and to live without my clothes being censored, especially by some school board who didn't know what was important to kids.

The day that this new rule was to be put into action, I wore my tank top in protest. News crews showed up at our school to talk to teachers and students to catch their reactions. I marched up to a reporter and started ranting about the injustice that was taking place in our schools. Later that day I was told to change, but I went home with a whole new outlook on life. I would dedicate my life to fighting injustices and standing up for what I believed in. Looking back, I must have sounded like quite the jackass. The school sent a letter of reprimand home but never enacted the anti-tube-top ban. It was my first political victory.

I took my activism to a whole new plateau with marijuana. I had a new lease on life. I was a freshman philosopher. My friends and I would sit around for hours smoking joints and talking about the meaning of life. I came to many good conclusions on life's mysteries as a result of these talks; they made me wiser. Weed is not like alcohol. The worst thing that comes from smoking is eating a little bit more and becoming a little lazier, whereas drinking booze can end in fighting, crying, or, even worse, alcohol poisoning. A lot of our smoking sessions ended with us blathering nonsense, but when we would grab on to a good theory about life, it was as if we brought a new positive energy into the world. We also decided that anything natural could not be bad for you.

Grade ten was uneventful until we learned about the marijuana march. This was what we needed, a day to pay our dues and stand up for our friend Mary Jane! We needed to be her soldiers. The march was supposed to be on "national pot day," which is known as "four/twenty" or April 20. Naturally, the march was a month later as the organizers had forgotten to book the route through downtown Toronto or the park where the speeches and drum circles would take place. My mom knew that my friends and I were planning to go to this march but surprisingly didn't protest my involvement. We were on really good terms, she and I, as we usually were around spring, when she actually saw me doing some schoolwork, which was only because I wanted to keep myself out of summer school. Maybe she knew she had to pick her battles or she would have ended up screaming 24/7. Whatever it was, she was remarkably quiet those days. So my girlfriends and I set out to fight for something we truly believed in: weed.

We marched with thousands of our brothers and sisters down the busiest street in Toronto, smoking joints, bongs, and pipes right in front of the city police, who, surprisingly, weren't doing a thing about it. I could have sworn I even saw a few smiling and cheering us on.

At one point, I got a little ahead of my friends as a result of smoking a joint with a Rastafarian man who was being interviewed by *High Times* magazine, when I accidentally walked right into a bike stand, flipped completely over it, and fell on my ass. When I raised my head, about fifty people reached out their hands to help me up. These were my people. No one laughed maliciously like "normal" people would when seeing someone fall. No one judged me.

At the end of the march everyone went to Queens Park, which is right in front of city hall. There we listened to speeches by fellow activists and the Green Party, a leftist political organization whose platform includes the legalization of marijuana, and who run in every federal election but for some reason never make it into power. For the rest of the afternoon my friends and I sat on a grassy knoll and smoked. We felt pretty darn good about ourselves and declared the day a success.

When I got home, my mom had just finished barbecuing chicken kabobs. She asked how the march had gone, and through a mouthful of souvlaki, I said, "I think we got a lot done."

She looked at me and rolled her eyes. I inhaled four kabobs and proceeded up to my room. I was feeling artistic, so I took out my paints and started decorating my bedroom fan. I drew an eye and a rainbow, and finished off my masterpiece with MAY 5TH WAS A GOOD DAY.

The marijuana march became a tradition for my friends and me, and we looked forward to it all year. When it finally came around again, we got all geared up. It would be our fourth march, and we were now mature eighteen-year-olds in grade twelve. The day proceeded the same as it had the year before. We were high and life was good. We returned to our grassy knoll and rolled joint after joint and did bong hit after bong hit. A photographer for the *Toronto Star* (one of the biggest papers in Canada) came up to our circle and asked me if he could take pictures of us smoking. I didn't put too much thought into it and said, "Sure." He sat beside me and started snapping away. We carried on, completely forgetting that he was there.

About two weeks later it was Mother's Day, and while I was struggling to throw a painting together for my mom, my brother busted into my room.

"Have you seen the newspaper today?"

At first I was mad that he hadn't knocked, then I grew somewhat curious as to why he would ask since he knew I never saw the paper.

"No. What did you get Mom? Can I put my name on it?"

He smiled in way that I knew meant he had something on me that could potentially be damaging.

"I got her flowers and a card, but after looking in the paper, I might just give her this."

He turned around the paper that he had been holding, revealing a large photo of yours truly exhaling an insane amount of smoke while gazing at the joint I had just taken a toke of. I was surprised to see that my profile looked as good as it did and was happy that the hood of my hemp sweatshirt was up. It added an extra something to the photo. I was quite proud of myself. My brother snatched it out of my hands.

"You're an idiot. I'm showing this to Mom."

Usually I wouldn't have cared, but it was Mother's Day. My mom didn't need to be reminded on her special day that her child was an asshole. What was I doing? Sure, I had done a lot of stupid things in my career of stupid things. But even I could see—perhaps for the first time—how ridiculously stupid this was.

On the plus side, this latest stunt wasn't going to involve the police calling my mom. And the caption under the photo did refer to me as a member of a group that was "striving to legalize marijuana for medical and recreational purposes." Heck, that was a step up from my days of fighting for tank tops in school, wasn't it?

I started planning my defense. I'd show her the newspaper before Ian could. I'd be casual about it, let her explode, then tell her she was overreacting. I knew the dance, could predict her every move.

I got dressed and headed downstairs to go to work—yes, that's right, I had a job, another plus on my side.

When I got to my family's Mother's Day brunch later that afternoon, I took a deep breath before entering the restaurant. I had already shown my mother the newspaper earlier that day and had assured her that chances were slim that any of the rest of the family would see it.

What unfolded at the restaurant shocked me. Not only had the entire family seen the paper, but they could not stop talking about it, ribbing me, laughing, and passing it around the table for every waiter, waitress, and busboy to see. What had happened to not airing your family's dirty laundry?

Through it all, my mother never said a word. I tried to laugh along—or laugh it off—with everyone else, but I found myself looking at her, trying to catch her eye. I don't know what I was hoping to find in her face or her expression.

She wasn't angry or disappointed. What I saw on her face as my aunts and uncles and brother taunted and teased was something closer to acceptance. Or maybe it was a surrendering of control. No matter. Like the protesters at the march that day, who had reached out their hands to help me off the ground, there was no judgment in her eyes. Her look seemed to say to me, *This is who you are right now, and I, my daughter, am just along for the ride.*

Chapter 17

Invisible

Joan

When Maddy was eighteen and still working at her restaurant job, I felt like I never saw her. At least compared to what we were used to. I missed her. So I decided at the last minute that it would be fun to have her come along on a business trip with me to London. I envisioned us enjoying the sites together and bonding like a mother and daughter should.

She was so excited with this news, she immediately set out to get time off from work, and of course, to organize her wardrobe. On the phone for hours on end, organizing various wardrobe trades with her girlfriends and talking incessantly about what she was going to do in London, she was determined to take the city by storm. Overhearing these conversations, I started to wonder if traveling with her was the best idea. AND, it suddenly occurred to me that the legal drinking age there was eighteen! I was going to be in meetings some of the time and was afraid I wouldn't be able to keep an eye on her the whole week. This could be a recipe for disaster. But it was too late to change my mind, so I doled out warning after warning about how I wasn't going to put up with any shenanigans from her while we were there.

I had never gotten into the habit of bringing my kids on business trips with me. I was afraid of them careening out of control in front of colleagues, as they were apt to do. I also wasn't a believer in traveling with them too far on vacation, for that matter. We had gone to the island of Montserrat years before for a sun holiday, but that been when they were still young and I could keep them under control—well, kind of. I also had made the mistake of taking them to Club Med in the Bahamas when Maddy was fifteen and Ian was eighteen. I'm crazy, I know. The two of them had themselves a fantastic time—without me. I was in my room most of the time, exhausted and watching TV, while the two maniacs indulged themselves in Bahama Mommas (the local drink), talent shows, dancing, and dating. Love was definitely in the air on that trip, just not for me. I swore after that vacation that I would never travel with them together again.

Maddy and I arrived at the airport for our trip to London with me looking like a slob (I usually travel in the closest thing to pajamas I can find) and Maddy looking like a supermodel. Maddy hates flying, so the flight wasn't exactly relaxing. She was white-knuckled the whole time, complaining that she couldn't get comfortable (poor baby) and moaning during the slightest bit of turbulence. Understand that when I fly, I try to turn my seat into my home—I have books, magazines, music, my work, and anything else I can bring along to make myself comfortable. After years of enduring a crazy travel schedule, I finally had it down to a science. Not Maddy. She had nothing to do for seven hours but make my life and our flight attendant's life miserable. She also can't sleep on planes, which I can do easily. Consequently, I ended up staying awake the whole flight, which I knew was going to mess me up since I had a meeting later the next day. But, I kept telling myself, we were together, and we were going to have a good time, and that's all that mattered.

When we arrived at Heathrow, I was exhausted. Maddy was excited. In a cab on our way to the city, Maddy oohed and aahed as she looked out the window at all the scenery and the spectacular palaces. One particular palace (I can't remember which one because I had my eyes closed) started her obsessing on how she wanted to meet Prince William. She thought she would make a great princess. I calmly explained to her that she would make a terrible princess. Princesses weren't allowed to go out partying whenever they felt like it, and they actually had to work hard.

When we got to the hotel, the real trouble began. The doorman practically fell over himself to make sure Maddy was being taken care of—he didn't give a damn about me, and I was the one who was paying! The concierge gushed over Maddy and asked her all kinds of questions. He also offered to give her any information or help she needed during her stay while ignoring me, the one holding the Visa card.

We got into our room and decided to take a nap before I

had my first meeting, which, fortunately, was being held downstairs in our hotel. I slept for a couple of hours and got up and showered while "Princess" continued sleeping. She said she was too jet-lagged to get moving yet. I explained that if she didn't get on the local clock, she would end up nocturnal the whole trip. She looked at me as though to say, *And why would that be a problem?*

I headed down to my meeting and got the usual indifferent service I was accustomed to receiving in this particular hotel. A couple of hours later Maddy appeared in the bar, looking like someone who had stepped out of a magazine. The hotel staff fell over themselves making sure she had everything she needed. This was the same staff that hadn't given a shit about me. What was going on? One waiter was so taken with our girl, he showered an embarrassing amount of attention on her. Maddy, of course, drank in her newfound popularity and, in particular, found our waiter "Marilyn" quite attractive. He was dark, broody, and a bit snarly—perfect! Over the course of the evening, a couple of my close friends came by to say hi and have a drink. None of us could believe the interest and the stir that Maddy was causing in the place. Maddy was in heaven—she was of the legal drinking age AND she was being catered to like a princess.

Later that evening, Maddy and I went out for a quiet dinner in the neighborhood. I wasn't up for much since I had gotten only a couple of hours sleep in the previous twenty-four hours and I was not as young as I used to be. Maddy, on the other hand, was feeling terrific after her extra long nap and was stoked about being in England.

The restaurant we chose was a bit more high-end than I would have liked. I wasn't throwing money around like a drunken sailor anymore since having my own company, but hell, why not treat the kid. You would think that if you were paying fifty million pounds for dinner you would be able to enjoy some privacy and one-on-one time. But not if you were with Maddy. As we were being seated, all eyes in the restaurant were on her. It was as if she were somebody famous.

We weren't at the table more than two minutes before two older gentlemen sitting at the next table leaned over and said hello to Maddy. What was up with this? They were a good ten years older than me, and I might as well have been invisible. It turned out they were major executives from one of the big British clothing chains and, within ten minutes of chatting up our girl, offered her their cards with a promise of some very special treatment whenever she wanted to visit one of their stores.

That night before turning in, I decided we should go for a night cap in the hotel bar before calling it a very long day. Marilyn was still working. He was beside himself that Maddy was back. The two of them chatted up a storm. I know when I'm not wanted, so I bailed and went up to the room. It was not late, but I told Maddy under no circumstances was she to be more than an hour. I couldn't spend the night waiting for her to come to bed. I was exhausted and had to work early the next morning.

I fell asleep within seconds of hitting the pillow but woke up with a jolt two hours later—no Maddy. I was furious. I called down to the bar, and sure enough she and Marilyn were enjoying a couple of drinks (free, thanks to Marilyn) and making some big tourist plans for the next day. I screamed into the phone at her and said she was not going to ruin this trip for me and if she valued her life at all, she would get her ass upstairs NOW. She did and promptly went to sleep. Thanks to the adrenaline shot, I couldn't get back to sleep for hours. I was starting to hate her and was still trying to figure out why everyone was looking at her so much over here.

The next couple of days went along much the same. Maddy slept every day until noon and stayed up all night. Or at least it felt like that to me. She and Marilyn were having a great time. He took her to all the usual touristy places and, most exciting for her, to the palaces. She was still hoping that somehow she could spot one of the princes. As if. When she and I did spend time together, people continued to stare at her on the street, in restaurants, in stores—it didn't matter where we were.

One night my good friends Nick and Peter, who are absolutely hilarious, invited us to have dinner with them and some other people at their favorite local restaurant. They told us that Jude Law ate there regularly, which was good enough for Maddy. The restaurant was pretty low-key and in a very posh area of London. You would think this would have been a safe bet for our little celebrity to stay out of trouble. Not quite. Within minutes of us all arriving, a somewhat inebriated middle-age man came up to the table and asked if Maddy would like to join him and his friends for a drink.

What the hell was wrong with these people? I'm her mother and clearly the people at the table with us were in my age-group. This guy felt just fine about openly hitting on my daughter in front of me!

Peter did not take too kindly to this. He looked as though he wanted to punch the guy. His boyfriend, Nick, however, was more fascinated with Maddy's newfound popularity. He suggested quietly to me that maybe we should be trying to make some money off the kid and put her in a reality show of her own. He wanted to call it *Maddy Downtown* and just follow her around with a camera and watch the commotion. After a couple of drinks, he decided that we should make Maddy dolls, develop a whole line of merchandise, and give her a percentage of the proceeds.

Over the course of the evening, we had several visitors at the table, or, I should say, Maddy did. Remarkable. After a couple of hours of this, Maddy decided that she was going to sit at the bar with some of her new friends (all male) and visit with the owners of the place. I thought Peter was going to have a heart attack, but Nick and I just carried on with our plans to build our "Maddy empire." By the time we left, Maddy had been offered a job by the owner and had been given countless business cards from all her new friends, with promises of dinner dates.

By the end of the week, I was finding the whole "Maddy the celebrity" bit tiring but was getting an idea of what it would be like to be famous. Horrible if you ask me. The last night we were there, we once again went for something to eat close to the hotel so that we (or at least I) could get to bed early for our flight the next day.

On our way to the restaurant, the straw finally broke this camel's back. A strange-looking man came up to Maddy on the sidewalk and reached out to touch her like she was some kind of goddamned priestess. Okay, that was it. I hauled off and swatted the guy away. I couldn't believe I had been reduced to this, but what was I supposed to do? Just let these lunatics paw at my baby?

As we were getting packed up later that night, I discovered that my baby intended to pack not one but three new "bongs" she had bought when she had been shopping. I had been aware of only one of these purchases, bought in Camden on one of the only shopping trips mother and daughter took together, but I hadn't considered at the time how she was going to get it home. So here we were. My patience had run out—I told her not only was she *not* going to bring the paraphernalia home but she was also going to wear sweats on the plane because I was done traveling with a celebrity.

The next day Maddy wore a hat and big sunglasses to the airport. No one could take their eyes off her. I consoled myself with the fact that at least I had prohibited her from packing her bongs but worried that the maid would find them in our empty room's wastebasket.

No worries, I told myself, you're almost home.

Boarding went smoothly, and as I was buckling my seat belt and settling in for our seven-hour flight, I turned to Miss Princess Diana to ask her what movie she wanted to watch.

She didn't answer me. I couldn't believe it, but she was asleep. Careful not to wake her, I gently removed her straw hat and fake Chanel sunglasses. She looked so young to me suddenly. So beautiful and, yes, I thought, happy.

CHAPTER 18

FIFTEEN MINUTES OF FAME

Maddy

When we landed in London, I instantly knew this was a city for me. It was busy and the vibe was hip. The first day I spent sleeping off my jet lag. The next day I put on my most fashionable outfit and headed out to shop till I dropped. I hailed a cab and asked the driver to take me to the shopping district. I walked around for hours, taking in the architecture and the fabulous stores. The first purchase I made was a beautiful hookah. I shopped all day and got some great clothes, too. I knew I would be way ahead of the fashion curve back home.

After I had dropped way too much of my money, I hailed a cab and hopped in. The driver asked me where I wanted to go when I realized I had no idea what my hotel was called. I sat for a minute trying to remember but drew a blank. I didn't have my cell phone with me, nor did I know the number to my mom's. I was completely lost. I did manage to find the key to my room but all it said on it was "Radisson." The cabbie informed me that there were about twenty of those in the London area. I told him to drive around until I recognized a landmark. In most cities I have been to, cabbies are not the most accommodating people. In London, however, the cabbies are the only friends you will need. This man started dialing the phone to every hotel asking if I was registered there. He didn't even have the meter on. He was genuinely concerned that I was a lonely Canadian, new to this metropolis. After about ten minutes of me deciding what bench seemed like a good one to sleep on and wondering where the Canadian embassy was, the man found my hotel. On the way there he explained the history of certain buildings. I couldn't believe the random kindness of this gentleman.

I fell in love with London a little more.

That night I met my mom and her friend for a drink in the bar. I was sporting my new London look, which consisted of my baggy black cargoes and a lace-up shirt. I felt pretty good about myself. The waiter, who was also the bartender, was cute but had a really bad attitude. He actually yelled at people. He would deny customers a certain drink if he didn't want to make it and scoffed at our wine choices. His accent told me he came from somewhere in Eastern Europe, which I thought explained his dark personality. We named him "Nazi." His real name was almost worse, Marilyn, which I guessed was a name common in his homeland, perhaps the equivalent of "Bob" in North America. For some reason, I was the only one he would take orders from. He and I started talking, and he told me that I was going to go out with him for a date that night. I didn't want to get yelled at, so I agreed to a date.

The beginning of the night was awkward. I asked him where he was from, and he told me that he was from Slovakia. I thought that since my dad's family is Estonian, we could bond over that, but all he had to say about Estonia was how ugly it was. I then asked if his country was nice and he just said no. I was reaching for anything we could talk about by this point. I told him how much I was enjoying London, but all he could talk about was how much he disliked it. The guy was definitely a half-empty kind of person. He took me to a bar in Soho that he disliked less than the others. We sat down, and he went to the bar to order drinks. I didn't even dare to ask for something specific and left the decision up to him. After about nine mojitos, he started loosening up. He was actually an interesting guy. He said his mom was a judge and told me a lovely tale of his car blowing up after someone rigged a bomb to it. There were a lot of good-looking English men there that I wanted to talk to but thought that would be a bad idea while with this guy.

We eventually started laughing and having a good time. Near the end of the night my phone rang. I picked it up and heard my mom yelling that it was three in the morning and that I better get back to the hotel right away. I hadn't realized that it was so late. We started walking back when he stepped in front of me and kissed me. We were making out in the street when the phone rang again. I ignored the call, and we kept walking to the hotel, stopping every couple of feet to kiss. What should have been a fifteen-minute walk ended up taking an hour. By the time we got back to the hotel, my cell phone was ringing off the hook. The guy from the front desk came out and cleared his throat. He told me that my mom had instructed him to tell me to go upstairs as soon as he saw me, and he told my date to go home. I said good-bye to the angry Slovakian and did the walk of shame up to the room. I stood outside the door and took a deep breath.

I opened the door to Mom yelling, "Where the hell have you been? This is not Toronto and you don't even know that guy. I have to work in the morning, and if you think this is how this trip is going to be, you can forget about it."

I apologized for interrupting her sleep and explained I had just lost track of time. My mom woke up early the next day while I continued to sleep until the afternoon. I had arranged to go out with the bartender again to see some sights. We met in the lobby and headed out the door. I put my arm out to hail a cab and he pushed it down. We argued for a while about taking a cab versus taking the bus. He won the fight and we got onto a double-decker. I know that it's part of the experience to take public transportation, but taking a cab just makes more sense time wise.

We went to the London Eye and spent way too much money on tickets. It was hot in the little capsule; I hated it. London is not a city of skyscrapers, so going so high seemed pointless to me. Without a drink, the angry Slovakian and I had nothing to say to each other. I wasn't attracted to his bad attitude anymore and wanted to push him off of the ride.

When the ride was finally over, he suggested that we walk to Buckingham Palace to check it out. I agreed to go, not realizing that the whole excursion would take three hours.

When I finally got back to the hotel, my mom was still out working, so I ordered room-service food and took a nap. She wasn't too pleased when she walked in to find me asleep. She figured I was still sleeping off the night before, but when I explained that I had been out all day with the angry Slovakian, I think she felt as though a day with him was punishment enough for my activities the night before.

The next night my mom and I went to dinner with two of her good friends in the posh area of Primrose Hill. I was excited about this dinner, as I was told that many of the British celebrities hung out in that area. We had a few cocktails, and as I went to the bar for another, I found myself surrounded by a group of Scottish guys. My mom came up and yelled at them to get away from me. She seemed a little stressed. She dragged me back to the table but the guys followed. They took a seat at our table and completely ignored my mom's wishes for them to leave me alone. My mom's friend, who knew the owner, asked that he tell the guys not to bother us. I started talking with the owner and was offered a job at the bar. I decided that I would move to London. Things seemed to come to me pretty easily there, so I figured it's where I belonged. I had a great evening, but was frustrated that I wasn't allowed to talk to any guys. It's hard to party and meet guys when you're eighteen and hanging out with your mom and her friends. That night my mom's friends told me about this place called Camden Town, which they described as a hippie market. I had to go. My mom and I decided we would go together because we hadn't spent much time with each other, between her working and me going out at night.

So to Camden we went the next day. I walked through a tunnel that consisted of scarves for walls. I couldn't hear my thoughts, let alone my footsteps. All I could smell were all sorts of different incenses burning as one. It was so pungent that I felt as though my nose hairs were burning. I didn't mind it, but my poor mom can't stand the smell of incense. She wasn't too pleased to be there from the beginning. As we walked deeper and deeper into the land of scarves, we began to see the people who dwelled in these tunnels. The people were more colorful than the scarves. The distinct sound of guitar, steel drum, and bass permeated the market. Little booths made the passageway tighter. The vendors sold pipes, bongs, posters, shirts, carvings, and jewelry. It was like heaven to me. Two Italian-looking men wearing matching suits and sporting mustaches danced to reggae in the middle of the aisle. They were smiling but their laughter seemed to disappear in the music. Guys would hiss in my ear, offering a smoke and an enhanced trip. I didn't need weed to get stoned, as I already felt like I was. It seemed like everyone there had a story to tell.

My mom, however, was freaking out. She was not into the claustrophobia or the people. She told me to hurry up and buy something so we could get out of there. I bought a poster of Bob Marley, Mick Jagger, and Peter Tosh sitting together laughing. I also purchased a bong and a pipe. She didn't think anything of the bong at the time because she was so focused on getting out of what seemed to be her own version of hell.

When it came time to leave London, I didn't want to go. I had fallen in love with the city, and it had fallen in love with me. My mom and I started packing our bags, but when it came to my various smoking instruments, she lost it. She said that it looked weird to bring back a bong, a pipe, and a hookah and that I was practically begging to be searched by airport security. I protested, explaining that there was no residue, but she stuck to her guns and made me leave my purchases behind. We left for the airport and I was a changed person. My time in London was the life I wanted permanently. I was treated like royalty there and was upset returning to Toronto where I couldn't even get a date.

At the airport, people were looking at me as if they were trying to figure out who I was. The fact that they were staring so aggressively may have been because I was wearing sunglasses and a hat. Whatever.

I was tired. It had been a whirlwind trip. I couldn't wait to get home and tell my friends all about it. Wait until they heard my stories.

I don't remember much about our flight home (I think I slept through all of it). But I do remember thinking as we waited to retrieve our baggage, before going through customs, that I was *grateful* my mom hadn't allowed me to pack that bong. It really wasn't necessary after all.

CHAPTER 19

OLD HABITS DIE HARD

Joan

Maddy has always had trouble with school. Some of it wasn't her fault, but by the time she was in high school, a lot of it was. By grade eleven she told me simply that school wasn't for her. I remember constantly trying to find ways to inspire her and sometimes even resorting to offering bribes.

By grade twelve, I discovered that she was skipping school constantly. When I arrived at one of her school's parents' nights, I was told by all of her teachers that they thought Maddy was really great, very smart, and a lot of fun—but that she was failing miserably.

There it was again. Everyone loved her, but that didn't translate into good marks. There was one teacher, however, who wasn't buying into Maddy's shtick. Unfortunately (or fortunately, depending on how you look at it), she was teaching

Maddy English. It was an important subject since Maddy was no longer taking any math or science courses, just a load of electives such as Man in Society and drama—stuff that, in my mind, wasn't going to lead anywhere. At the very least, students need a final year English credit to get into any university across the country. But what bothered me the most was that Maddy was actually good at English. Her essays, when she did them, were excellent. Her research was impeccable, and her thought process was more mature than that of most kids her age. Heck, she had majored in debate with me for years.

At this point in my life, it had been a year and a half since I had quit smoking and I had recently been dumped by a guy who I thought was the man of my dreams. I was heartbroken, menopausal, but at least, I told myself, nicotine-free. What's more, I was skinny and running about twenty-five miles a week. When I started exercising after quitting smoking, I couldn't run for more than a minute. But now, as a cigarette ad once declared, I had come a long way, baby, and was taking my newfound good health very seriously. I was also trying to find my "more tranquil self" and had filled my bedroom with Enya CDs, a fountain, and every self-help book I could find under the sun.

Truth be told, I'd never been tenser, really, but thanks to my self-help books, at least I could define my stress, ponder it, and then, of course, attempt to empty it from my mind.

In between running, I practiced yoga and was able to do stuff I'm convinced I will never be able to do again, like hanging from a door jamb, upside down. Simply put: I was having a midlife crisis. Anyone around me, I'm sure, would have bought me a pack of cigarettes and a bottle of Scotch if they thought I would have gone for it.

My new business was doing reasonably well and wasn't causing me horrible stress. The office that Suzanne and I rented was just up the street from the house. My travel had gone from once a week to every couple of months, which at one point Ian confessed to me, he found disappointing. He didn't say it to be mean, but rather explained that he and Maddy had found their groove without me, and they just had to adjust to my new, constant presence. I didn't take it personally. I was intent on renovating my body and making sure my kids were being served up plenty of love. I was around and that's all that mattered.

But back to Maddy and her schooling, which was becoming my obsession. I rode her mercilessly—especially about her English course. I got her a tutor who came once a week. A very bright and lovely girl, he kept telling me. She'll be just fine.

As we came into spring, I noticed that Maddy didn't seem quite as focused on her schoolwork, as she should have been, so I was right there to nail her. She got defensive and argued that she was on top of her game. She asked me when was I ever going to be happy with who she was becoming? Couldn't I give her a little credit just once?

About a month later it became clear that her academics were taking a dive and that she was in no way on top of her game. I got a call from her English teacher who said there would be no way Maddy would pass the class. She was eighteen and wasn't going to be able to graduate. I couldn't breathe.

I sat down with Maddy that afternoon and told her what her teacher had said, and she looked at me with relief. She explained to me that she really wasn't interested in getting a high school diploma. Instead she was looking into the concept of "self-education." Okay, now I had heard it all. What the hell was she going to do—just hang out watching the Discovery Channel? She said that, as a matter of fact, you can learn a ton from television and that it's a shame it gets a bum rap.

What was she talking about? I was going to lose it. Breathe.

Maddy spent the next few days away from me as much as possible, working as many shifts at her part-time job as she could get. The school discussions were not going well. She was refusing any suggestion that she retake her final year again the next fall and redo failed courses. She said it was bad enough to be one year older than the other kids, but she refused to be two years older.

"Tough shit," I wanted to scream. I kept doing my yoga, but once again I wanted to kill her.

She explained that after her fellow classmates graduated, she would continue working at the restaurant for a few months, and then she was going to travel across Europe. This was going to be her first semester of self-education. After all, traveling around the world was way better than sitting in a classroom in Toronto. This was her logic.

I decided to take a step back. I had to figure out a way to communicate better with her. One day I dropped by the restaurant where she was working. It was a slow day at the office, and Suzanne and I were in the mood for lunch. I woke up with a bad feeling about Maddy that morning, but dismissed the maternal ESP and told myself I was being paranoid. She was still attending classes, or at least I thought she was, and I still thought we had a fighting chance for her to secure at least a couple of credits.

When Suzanne and I got to the restaurant, one of Maddy's friends who was also employed there looked panicked. I knew in that moment that Maddy wasn't even working there anymore. Sure enough, after interrogating the poor girl, I learned that Maddy had staged a very dramatic exit about a week before. She told her boss that he was objectifying all the young girls working there. He basically agreed that he was and asked her to get the hell off his property. Hmmm. I was torn between rage and pride. With Suzanne by my side, I hunted Maddy down like a bloodhound and eventually found her at her other girlfriend's house. I started to scream bloody murder.

So much for breathing.

She started crying and told me the whole story of her termination.

Evidently, Maddy was sick and tired of her boss telling the waitresses to look sexy and to smile at the handsome customers. She said it felt as though he was using them as prostitutes to pull in business. As much as I don't necessarily agree with this particular approach to business development, she had gone into the job with her eyes wide open. The restaurant was known to be a well-established and respectable pick-up joint, and let's face it, Little Miss Gloria Steinem knew that when she signed on. Still, I was proud of her thinking and her ideals but furious with the fact that she had been lying to me for over a week.

After my tirade, she promised that she would get a new job and focus even more on her schooling. What I didn't know at the time was that her whole school year was already a wash. We received the report card a couple of weeks later. She had not passed one single course. And on top of all of this, she was adamant that she was not going to return to school—ever. In the words of my Romanian hairdresser: "Just cut a vein."

A couple of unemployed months went by, and Maddy sunk deeper and deeper into the couch. Anybody else who lay around that much would be diagnosed with depression at the very least, but Maddy enjoys doing nothing—or at least used to. I have to be honest, I was one lazy teenager myself, so I understood on some level. But even Miss Lazy was starting to understand that no education and no job equaled a bad life. She had nothing to talk about and was not meeting anyone new.

Maddy and I had always enjoyed taking long drives into the country on a weekend afternoon. We would chat, listen to music, and do a little shopping in small towns. We had an unwritten agreement during these drives: We wouldn't talk about anything that would lead to conflict. But not this one particular drive. I had a plan. I had been watching her closely and noticed that she was getting weak. She was starting to question her decisions and was slowly realizing that not only was the cross-Europe trip not going to happen, but neither was anything else. Time to hit. "Let's go for a ride," I said one Sunday afternoon, and she agreed, so we both jumped into the car.

I had her trapped—which was the way I liked her. I started up about the school thing and how, honest to God, she was going to be completely screwed without a high school diploma. Any self-respecting potential employer would look at that and wonder why a kid like her was a dropout. She had every advantage known to woman, and she had turned her back on all of it, and that's how the world was going to see it. She started to break. She said that a couple of her friends were going back to school for the winter semester. I dived in with a promise that we would find just the right school for her and that I was willing to pay whatever tuition was necessary. Maddy, being Maddy, decided it might be fun to go to a boarding school where they had horses and uniforms and fun stuff like that. I explained to her that she was a little long in the tooth for boarding school and that she needed to get her head out of the clouds.

I managed to find out about this tiny little school on the same street as my office (and just up the street from home). This place was a trip. The school was run by a middle-age hippie who went by the name of Harvey Rainbow. I still don't know if that was his real name, but I didn't care. Harvey was a character, but it seemed we had found the best place for Maddy. He was just offbeat enough that it might work. There were only twenty students in the whole school. If this wouldn't be enough attention, then nothing would be. I still had to convince the little derelict that returning to school would be the only thing that could save her from a life of working at a take-out window, or worse, of me supporting her.

She agreed and that fall started her final year of school—

all over again—with a zeal I'd never seen in her. She visited my office during her breaks and at lunch to tell Suzanne and me about all the stuff she was learning. I was so pleased and impressed with the quality of work Maddy was cranking out.

Amazing.

She was taking charge of the student body and helping design a fashion curriculum for the school as a side project. Go figure! She had found her footing with a guy that answers to "Rainbow."

By the end of the school semester, Maddy was shining in her studies. She was in her room the entire last month of the semester, working away on projects and assignments.

That spring Maddy graduated. The school hosted a special dinner, and since there were only ten or so graduates, it was an intimate gathering, complete with awards, speeches, and toasts.

Maddy looked so beautiful that night sitting at a table with her fellow students at the front of the room. I couldn't help smiling at the memory of her, way back when, in grade school, sitting at her special desk next to the teacher. She always seemed to get the front-row seat.

I learned that night that not only had Maddy graduated (sorry, but old habits die hard and I was holding my breath on that one) but that she had also graduated with high honors.

"Surprised?" another mom, who was sitting next to me, whispered into my ear.

"Not really," I said. "Just relieved."

And then I really remembered to breathe.

CHAPTER 20

THE FOURTH DIMENSION

Maddy

After four months of working part-time as a waitress and fail-ing my final year of high school, I had to fess up to the fact that once again I didn't have all the answers. I had been skipping school and at one point had even tried convincing myself and my mother that I would be better off homeschooling myself. I told my mom that I didn't believe in the educational system and that its only function was to turn kids into societal robots. I argued that with self-education, I could learn about what was important to me and the world at large. I could teach myself about civil rights, for example, and how to effectively fight for what was right. She stared at me blankly, as if I had lost my mind. I also told her that I had no intention of ever going to college.

Instead, I continued working at the restaurant, hoping to

save up enough money to move to London. Four months after starting the job, I realized that not only was I not saving any money, but I was also spending more than I made on having a good time. When all of my friends started going off to college at the end of the summer, I felt lonely. At one point I thought that I would go to my friend Molly's college and live with her. She needed moral support and I needed a vacation. Determined to hatch my new plan, one day during the busiest time of year, when the Toronto film festival was going on, I walked up to my manager and asked him to fire me. He said that there was no way that he was going to do that seeing as how I was the best hostess he had at the time. I called my friend Tina and asked what I should do. She told me that quitting was probably the best choice. I got off the phone and told my manager that I was quitting. He told me to grab my stuff and get out. Furious, I went down to the basement where the staff kept their belongings.

Two minutes later the owner walked in and, pretending I wasn't there, said to the room, "Some people are quitters in life, and we should feel sorry for them because they will amount to nothing."

As I left, my whole body shook with adrenaline. I walked outside where my two fellow hostesses were standing and told them what had happened. The owner came outside and put his arms around the two girls.

"These are my girls and my bar, so get off the property. We don't want people like you around."

I thought that was a little harsh, but more important,

wanted to prove that none of us were "his girls."

"We aren't yours, and I'm proving that to you right now by leaving."

I felt as though a battle had been won, but as I walked away, tears welled up in my eyes. I bit my cheeks. I didn't want to cry as a result of that asshole's comments. I wouldn't give that to him. The next two days I pretended to go to work so that I could avoid getting in trouble with my mom. I would get dressed for the job and go over to a friend's house until my supposed shift was over. I would tell tales of bad and good customers to my mom when she would ask how my day was. I almost got away with it until my mom decided to show up with Suzanne for lunch one day. My friend Ella, who I had gotten hired, greeted my mom. When Mom asked where I was, Ella broke down and told her that I had not been working there for days.

I was chilling out at my friend's when my mom and Suzanne pulled into the driveway. My mom asked what I was doing there, and I told her that I had gotten off work early. She told me that she knew I had quit and started yelling and really losing it. I felt so humiliated and angry and lost. What did she care? I was failing at everything.

Before I knew it, things went from bad to worse, and I was screaming back at her and calling her names. I snapped and told her to "fuck off."

I never swore at my mom and was about to find out why. She went to smack me across the face, but I flinched and she ended up palming me in the nose. What happened next was complete insanity. I saw myself doing it but couldn't stop my body from moving. I shoved her. She stumbled down a step or two, then stood there in shock. I didn't move. Realizing what I had just done, I booked out the front door. I ran down the street for my life. I got on a bus and sat, totally shocked. I couldn't believe what I had just done. I met up with Molly and cried. Molly is not the best person to cry around as she gets really uncomfortable. She suggested we get a bottle of vodka and talk about it. We sat in the park for the remainder of the day and drank. At dusk we saw headlights driving through the park. We thought it was odd but ignored it. As the car approached, we realized it was the police. All I could think was how perfect this was; now I was going to be arrested for being underage and drinking in public. The police, as it turned out, were looking for a criminal but asked what we were doing. I explained what had happened with my mom, and all he said was, "Wow, you better call and apologize." I knew he was right. I called my mom, who had gone to my aunt's, and told her how sorry I was. She apologized too, and we made up. She told me we would have to have a talk when she got home the next day, which I agreed to.

The next day we went on one of our drives. My mom and I did this almost every weekend. We liked hitting the open road and seeing different towns. We usually got a lot figured out on our little trips. On this particular drive, however, she had an agenda. She had trapped me in the car and started in on me about going back to school to get my diploma and going on to college. I knew she was right. I wanted to finally take control of my life in a positive way; I just didn't know how.

Taddle Creek was an alternative school consisting of twenty

students from grade nine through grade twelve. The head of the school was a man named Harvey Rainbow. He and I hit it off from day one. I was really in my hippie stage then. He thought I would be an excellent addition to the school. He was a philosopher like me, and believed that any kid could do well given the right encouragement and the right environment. I needed seven credits, which Harvey assured me he could help me get if I committed to doing what it took. I committed to the school, and, with threats from my mom of what would happen if I did badly, committed to myself to do well. This was my last chance, so it was good that I was in Last Chance High as I liked to call it. Most of the students were there for a reason. Either they couldn't do well in a regular school environment or they had screwed up at a previous school.

I started in and quickly adjusted. I had been out of school for six months, so I had a newfound appreciation for it. Learning beat working at some shitty restaurant. My first semester I did very well, which encouraged me. Most of my classes consisted of an average of five kids, but my creative writing class was just me by my lonesome. This school was my answer. The teachers knew me on a personal level and respected me as an adult, as long as I respected them and acted like an adult. The students would get a talking-to if they were not doing what they should be, but otherwise they were left alone. We could take breaks when we wanted, eat when we wanted, and use the bathroom when we wanted. The school treated us like human beings. The staff at Taddle Creek consisted of Connie (Harvey's wife), Alex, and Theresa. They were there because they loved to teach.

For once in my life I enjoyed walking into school, because I would be appreciated for my talents and my individuality. I was changing, I could actually feel it. I would often have one-on-one philosophical talks with Harvey, who cared about what I had to say. During spring semester, a few kids graduated and the school got a little smaller. At that point, I had gotten really interested in fashion. Two others also wanted to take a fashion course. I brought it up with Harvey, and he gave me the go-ahead to design a fashion curriculum. I set up projects and tests as well as our exam. I aced the course.

In the middle of the semester, Harvey called me into his office to have a talk. I wasn't used to going into offices and not getting in trouble, so I was taken aback when he handed me a medallion with a dude and a baby on it. I was puzzled. He explained that he gives Saint Christopher medals to students who exemplify good leadership at the school. I had never been praised for being a good example before. He went on to tell me that I was a fourth-dimensional kind of person. I had no idea what this meant. When I asked him for an example, he told me that Chris (another Taddle Creeker) was also one. He said a fourth-dimensional person was someone who knew what life was really worth and who knew the important things and who had more insight than the average person. I still wasn't really clear on what in God's name he was talking about, so I asked for another example of this "fourth-dimensional person."

"Martin Luther King," he said.

I could not believe that he was comparing me with Martin Luther King. I was put to shame by this comparison. He told me that I had the potential of greatness that many people do not have and that I had a responsibility to do great things and that sitting idly by would be a huge injustice on my part. I left his office completely flattered but also feeling a bit uneasy. Not only would I now have to do extremely well on my exams, but I would also have to do extremely well in life.

When I told my mom the date of my graduation, I could have sworn I saw her eyes tear up. Taddle Creek graduations take place at a restaurant where all of the graduating students and their parents have dinner followed by diplomas and speeches.

It was the first time in my life that I felt like I belonged, that I had earned something. Sitting with my friends listening to those speeches, I didn't feel like a rebel or a juvenile delinquent or a princess. I felt like I deserved to be there. Like somehow, in some way, I had reached another dimension.

CHAPTER 21

BEING THERE

Joan

The summer after Maddy graduated, I decided to rent another cottage with her and my best friend, Heather, for a couple of days of rest and relaxation away from the city. I got there first due to my schedule and waited for my girls to arrive.

Maddy had fortuitously grabbed a ride with Heather, so they had had a few hours of intimate catch-up time in the car. It turned out that Maddy had spent most of that time telling Heather all about her new boyfriend, Lawrence. I was aware of Larry (as we called him) and knew that he was twenty-eight, worked at a skateboard shop, and used one as his means of transportation, which gave Ian and me a good laugh. Most important though for Maddy, was the fact that he was really, really good-looking. She was the envy of her friends. What more does any self-respecting nineteen-year-old need?

I could never have been prepared for what ensued. The morning of the ride to the cottage, Maddy's friend had called her and identified Larry as a guy who had previously infected a close family friend of hers with HIV!

HIV.

Maddy's friend was pretty sure, but not 100 percent sure, so Maddy was waiting for a call from her to confirm it, and we joined the vigil.

Something happens to me in these situations that is really hard to explain. I guess it's a form of shock or some kind of defense mechanism. I get calm to the point where I seem like I don't care. I become convinced that everything will work out just fine and I express that to everyone around. I get aggravated by anyone who expresses worry or tries discussing the problem in any way other than light and breezy—I guess they call it denial. Several hours later I find myself alone with what I can describe only as a gaping, awful hole and an overwhelming level of fear. I don't generally express this fear to anyone except maybe to my sister, Kim. After the fact. Meanwhile I live inside of this terror that is just so damned gripping. I know from firsthand experience that things don't "always turn out for the best" or "happen for a reason" or any of those platitudes we feed ourselves when really bad shit is going on. My brother, at the age of twenty-six, was so completely overcome with mental illness that he killed himself. Bad things do actually happen and there is not always a good ending. That event early in life has served to create an underlying fear in me, especially concerning my kids, that has been pretty hard to shake.

Maddy is the greatest girl in the world and my baby, so the idea of her not sticking around because of some grimy little schmuck made me so sick and crazy I couldn't see straight. And on the more shallow side of things, there went another holiday.

I had assumed that Maddy had had sex with this guy, because I had picked her up there one morning after they spent the night together. She was nineteen, and I wasn't naive enough to think she wasn't sexually active. I had asked her if she was practicing safe sex (a topic largely unexplored by my kids and me until recent years), and she assured me that she had not had sex with him and ended with a strong "please let's not talk about this." I trusted Maddy when it came to sex. This was different though—she really liked the guy, plus she had spent overnights with him, something she had not openly done with anyone before. I hoped that if she had become sexually active with Larry that she was being safe. I also have never been a big believer in badgering the kids about this beyond the occasional warning because they have had sex education jammed down their throats at school since the early days. They are either going to listen or not. Nothing I was going to say was going to guarantee sensible, responsible behavior. At that stage in their lives, I was lucky that they were talking to me at all, so listening and obeying was a totally different ball game.

The next several hours were endured as if in a torture chamber. Maddy assured me right off the bat that she had not had sex with Larry, and, if anything, she had been questioning why he was holding back. She, like any self-respecting teenage girl, thought he just wasn't into her, but as it turns out, there was this little detail he wasn't sharing. She had even asked him if he had ever had an HIV test (God bless her), and he answered "not that long ago," which, although it was technically the truth, was not exactly the right answer. This guy was disgusting and I hated him!!!!!!!

We had an evening with Heather at the cottage with some wine, a barbecue, and obsessive conversation centering on Lawrence, AIDS, and bad old society. Maddy was upset. Even though she hadn't had sex with this creep, they had slept in the same bed, shared a toothbrush, and kissed—all this activity without him saying one goddamned word. I fantasized about showing up at his workplace on a skateboard, with a ghetto blaster blaring the theme song from *Philadelphia*, set on repeat. We talked into the wee hours of the morning. The next morning Maddy's friend called from Toronto and informed her that indeed this was the same guy—an absolute positive ID.

Whoa . . . Maddy was sobbing and incredibly freaked out, realizing that if she had had sex, this could have killed her. She was still scared that she may have gotten the virus somehow, but luckily, Heather, being a high school counselor, had all kinds of encouraging things to say to put her at ease. My little girl! I swear I wanted to go and give this guy some real trouble. I don't know why I think I'm Don Corleone, but mess with the tykes and Crazy comes out to play.

My mother arrived the next day, which meant she was pulled into the drama. My cell phone was ringing every five minutes with calls from Maddy's posse of girlfriends freaking out and planning Larry's demise. Maddy put on a brave front in spite of everything. We decided she needed to have an HIV test right away. We toyed with the idea of reporting this guy to the police even though he hadn't done anything (technically, anyway) to put her in harm's way. In retrospect, this incident marked the beginning of our being able to talk openly about sexual issues and men—I mean, this was as raw as it could get. Or so we thought.

After a few more days of angst and drama, I decided we should surrender and head home and forget about the remaining days of the holiday, so down to the city we went. I wasn't exactly relaxing all that much anyway.

Maddy and a couple of her friends were hanging at the house, and somehow Maddy got just fired up enough to lob a call to Larry. His response to her statement that she knew he was HIV positive was astounding—he didn't feel it was really any of her business and "it wasn't something he told just anyone." When she shot back with "we made out and slept in the same bed," he told her that she was never someone he felt he was having a relationship with, so what was the problem? Once again she was upset, but she decided to try her best to forget about it, get the HIV test, and move on from there. I was so blown away by the whole thing that I had a hard time not calling him myself.

A couple of weeks later Maddy had her test and all was fine. But her friend's friend (the one infected with HIV), after hearing Maddy's story, decided this shitbag had done enough damage. She reported him to the police herself.

A couple of weeks later Suzanne arrived at work at my house one morning and asked if the HIV carrier Maddy had been dating (of course she had heard the whole story) was named "Lawrence." When I answered yes, she informed me that his face was plastered all over the news and there was a warrant out for his arrest. This was getting crazier by the minute. Sure enough, there he was on all the news reports as the guy who was suspected of infecting not one but THREE girls with HIV—all of them younger than he. I got Maddy out of bed and told her that lover boy was a wanted man.

The phone lines lit up all over again. The drama factor with the girls was completely over the top. Maddy decided that she should offer up her story to the police. I'm not going to lie when I tell you that my first instinct was to say "not a chance" since I didn't want this sociopath coming after her (he had slept at our house for God's sake!). She was surprised that I didn't want to help these girls out and build a stronger case against Larry. Just the fact that we were having conversations about police, district attorneys, and building cases was freaking me out. It was getting too creepy for me. Maddy really was trying to do the right thing, which I was proud of, but too damn bad.

Maddy argued that it would be incredibly reckless for her not to do anything, and shit, didn't I trust her judgment? I gently pointed out that the guy she thought was soooooooooo fabulous was knowingly infecting others with HIV, so maybe her judgment wasn't quite as good as she thought. She told me that she had had a weird feeling about him right from the beginning. She explained that there was always something a bit off about the guy, which was one of the reasons she hadn't had sex with him. After a lengthy debate, she convinced me that talking to the police was the right thing to do.

She got the name of the police detective in charge of the Sexual Crimes Unit—again a world you don't want to know about unless you're watching TV or reading a James Patterson book—and before you could say "I'm a murderer," she had a meeting set up "downtown."

In the meantime Larry had been captured and put into a holding facility to wait for a preliminary hearing. The word from the police was that he was completely nonverbal, refused to answer any questions, and didn't have a lawyer—CREEPY! Keep in mind, this whole story was breaking all over the news because his case is precedent-setting in Canada and the charges of aggravated assault for something like this are the result of fairly new legislation.

I took Maddy down to police headquarters to meet the detectives. They had her on camera and asked her a couple of preliminary questions, then asked me to get lost (they didn't say it like that, but you know what I mean), so I did. I went shopping to take my mind off the fact that my daughter came so close to getting a terminal disease from a guy who was now in jail and all over the news and that she was now sitting with a couple of seasoned Sexual Crimes Unit detectives discussing the matter. On top of everything else, the shopping in the area sucked, I had just started smoking (yet again), and I was burned out because Larry had ruined my summer holiday.

Now as I write this, Larry is out on bail and living north of the city. His trial is pending. If he is convicted, he will spend several years in jail. If not, he will be free to roam around and hang with whomever he wants.

As much as I hate Larry and all that he caused in my life, he marked a turning point in my relationship with Maddy.

We saw eye to eye on something. We banded together and weathered a storm. Scared and traumatized, she reached out to me, and I was there.

Thank God, I was there.

CHAPTER 22

GETTING TESTED

Maddy

I have been single for most of my dating life. That's not to say that I didn't have interest from boys. In fact, I had a lot, but I never settled down and committed to dating any of them. I have high standards for relationships. When I met Larry, I thought that he fulfilled all of those standards. He was gorgeous, in fact, too much so. One has to question the balance of power with a guy that is prettier than you, but I was not about to complain. I met him at a bar downtown while celebrating a friend's birthday. I knew I had to have him the moment that I saw him. He was hip, with a great sense of style, and he skateboarded. I was hooked like a dumb-ass fish biting on a fake lure. Who cared if he was twenty-eight and I was nineteen?

I initiated the flirting ritual, but the next week he called exactly when he said he would. I was shocked. I wondered why this guy was so eager, but chalked it up to him seeing just how fabulous I was, which, for some reason, most guys seemed to miss. I started to question whether the beer goggles were thick the night that I met him. I decided to meet up with him out of curiosity. I dragged three of my best girlfriends along just in case. They were hoping that he would be a dog so that they would have some teasing material, but boy, were they disappointed. The look on their faces was priceless when this movie star of a guy walked up and gave me a big hug. I grinned at them from over his perfect shoulder. I was proud to be with him.

After a few hours I learned that not only was this guy perfect to look at but he was also smart and funny. I thought surely that would be our last meeting because there was no way that I was that lucky. I had the chance that night to sneak off with my friend Kate and ask what she thought. Asking your friend's opinion is a dangerous game. You could be falling for a guy, but one negative word from a friend and it sticks with you. I have broken up with many a great guy as a result of negativity from the judges. Kate agreed that he was great.

Larry and I kissed that night but nothing more. We continued to date after that. Every time I saw him, I fell for him more and more. On our third date, he asked if I wanted to sleep at his house. I paused and thought. I knew that the chances of us ending up in a relationship would severely drop if I slept with him, but I was still dying to go. I was in a jam. I said that yes, I would sleep at his place but that I wouldn't have sex with him, so if he wasn't into that, then I would go home. When he said that he wouldn't be so crass to assume I would have sex with him, I liked him even more.

We didn't have sex that night, but I started staying at his place more and more often, and even told my mom that I was there. I didn't want to lie to her anymore.

It was the summertime, and Larry and I had suddenly started drifting apart. A month went by without talking to him before I worked up the nerve to call. We got together a few times after that, but I started seeing him for who he really was. He was dark, but I didn't understand why. I figured the strain between us was because I didn't have sex with him and wasn't behaving the way that he wanted me to. This is not to say that I was behaving badly, but I was not on his same wavelength. I often said the wrong thing. Teasing him was not acceptable. I think of myself as a strong person who is sure of who I am. Instead of being confident in my decisions and actions, he made me re-evaluate who I was and tore down my confidence. I thought going out with such a good-looking guy would do the opposite. I ignored those feelings and tried to keep up with him. After all, he was older and wiser.

One night when we were making plans to meet up, I begged him to wear the vintage Blue Jays hat that looked so good on him. I often asked him to wear the hat, especially when we were going to see my friends. As it turned out, that hat saved my life. We went out for a couple of drinks before going over to my friend's house. That's when dark Larry came out. Someone made a comment about sex, as nineteen-year-olds often do, when he yelled across the room, "Maddy wouldn't know anything about that since she hasn't put out."

I was so embarrassed to be hanging out with such an asshole. My friends were looking at me awkwardly, like, "Nice guy."

I defended him that night. I had told Kate that she and her boyfriend could sleep at my house since my mom was out of town, and I gave her the key. This, too, would be one of the luckiest decisions that I have ever made. I had decided earlier in the evening that tonight I was going to make the move and finally have sex with him. I was quite drunk when we got to my place, which meant I had liquid courage to make the first move. My mood was the opposite of how you want to feel around a guy that you have been seeing. I was not comfortable with him or myself. I had lost who I was somewhere between his looks and talent at manipulation.

We went to my room and started fooling around when I asked him if he had a condom. He didn't have that same excited look on his face that other guys usually do when they know it's a sure thing. He simply said that he didn't.

Then I asked him, "When was the last time you were tested?"

"Awhile ago," he said.

"Then we're not going to have sex."

The morning started like any other: with him trying to escape as soon as he could and me feeling awkward. Thankfully, Kate was there to break the ice. I went straight to see her in the back room of my house as Larry got his things together. I was still proud to be a part of his life and have him be a part of mine. I couldn't see past his blindingly good looks. He beckoned from the front room for me to join him, so that I might have the privilege of walking him to the bus stop. I told him to come back and say hi to Kate. He walked to the top of the three steps that led down to the room and said a cold, quick hi. I looked at Kate in hopes of seeing that look on her face like the first time she had met him, when she was in awe of his beauty, but instead I saw her look as though she had seen a ghost. He turned and walked away, and I looked at her with panic.

"Kate, what's wrong?"

She asked a very specific question that scared me even more: "Maddy, did you sleep with him last night?"

I told her I had not, but I wondered why she was asking. I had to walk him to the bus stop, so I didn't have time to get a story out of her. All she instructed me to do was ask him if he knew Marie. I kept asking why, but she just kept on repeating the question I was to ask him. I was shaking when I met him at the front door. I started walking him to the bus stop and went over the question I was to ask him again and again in my head. I didn't know what it was regarding, but I knew it couldn't be good. I didn't know if I wanted to know. He then realized that he had left his wallet by the bed, and we turned around to get it. He grabbed it and told me that I didn't have to walk him back. I said fine and gave him half-assed directions, practically closing the door in his face. I ran back to Kate. She asked me if I had asked him if he knew Marie. I told her that he said no, he didn't know her. I don't know why I lied. What Kate said next would ring in my ears and stay with me for life.

"Larry has HIV and is the one who gave Embem HIV." Embem is what all of us knew Marie as. We all knew the story of Embem.

I started to cry. I cried out of relief and I cried out of fear. How could this be happening to me? Kate started to cry with me. All she said was how sorry she was. I looked up at her and said, "You better be damn sure about this, Kate, because we aren't talking about a cold here." She spent that day trying to get in touch with Marie with no luck. I asked her why she hadn't known this when she first met him, and she told me that the Blue Jays hat was the same hat that he had worn when she met him through Marie. It's strange how little, insignificant details can change your life. If he hadn't been wearing that hat, I wonder to this day if things would have been different.

Two days later I drove up to our cottage with Heather (my mom's best friend), and I told her what had happened. I was worried about telling my mom—not because I didn't want her to know the truth, but because I didn't want to scare her. My mom was very calm about the whole situation though, telling me that it probably wasn't the same guy and that even if it was, I had nothing to worry about. I don't know what it is about moms, but just hearing "everything will be fine" is all you need in order to believe that it actually will be.

The day that Nanna came up to the cottage is when the shit hit the fan. Kate called late in the afternoon and told me that she had heard from Marie. Larry was HIV positive. Marie had confirmed Kate's belief. My heart sank, my ears rang with blood, and I thought that I was going to faint. I didn't talk to her long because I thought that I was going to be sick. I went back to the table where my mom and Heather were sitting with Nanna, enjoying the warm evening air. I sat there for a second as they chatted away before breaking down into hysterical sobs. I hadn't cried like that since I was a kid. I couldn't get any words out or hardly breath. I mustered up all of the air I could and blurted the words I feared saying: "Larry has HIV." My mom, always strong, reassured me that I would be fine. She knew that I hadn't slept with him and therefore hadn't had an opportunity to be infected.

Soon after that day, I went back to the city with my mom and we talked the entire ride home. Once home we decided I would call Larry and confront him about what I had heard. My whole body started shaking as soon as he picked up the phone.

"Hey, how are you? How was the cottage?"

He had no idea what was about to happen to him.

"Are you HIV positive?"

The silence on the other end felt like it lasted an eternity. His voice quickly turned cold and hollow. "Why?" was all he had to say.

I asked him if the name Marie rang a bell, and all he could say was yes. I asked the question again. He then admitted that he was indeed infected with the virus. My body was shaky, but my voice stayed strong.

"Why didn't you tell me?"

"I don't tell every person that comes up to me on the street."

At this point I knew that I was dealing with a person that I didn't know or want to know for that matter. I talked to him for another two minutes, continuously asking why he hadn't told me. He was mean and cold. I explained that having someone sleep in his bed usually constitutes a relationship greater than one he'd have with some random person on the street. We had a lot of silent moments. When I finally realized that this guy wasn't going to give me any answers, I got off the phone. The severity of what I was dealing with was too much. What I was feeling was probably only a fraction of what this guy was going through, having to live with this disease and facing a death sentence. I called him back. He didn't pick up the phone but I left him a message anyway.

"Hi, I'm sorry about my reaction, it just caught me off guard, and in the middle of all of this, I didn't ask how you're dealing with everything. I'm sorry that this has happened to you, and if you ever need to talk to someone about it, you can call me." He didn't deserve me being nice to him, but no one deserves HIV.

The next week Marie called me. She had gotten my number from Kate and wanted to talk to me about the whole situation. She had decided to report Larry to the police. She felt a sense of responsibility for what could have happened if I had slept with him. She told me her story about how she had dated him for a long while, how he had told her he loved her, and how eventually they had stopped using condoms. She contracted the virus. He tried to convince her to stay with him so that they could go through it together. He said that he didn't know that he had it, but she found out through the AIDS clinic that he had been going there for years. She didn't press charges at the time. I understood. She had already gone through so much at such a young age and was forever changed. She then told me that she would appreciate if I would talk to the police to help build the case against Larry. I talked to my mom about it. She had some reservations, but I had already made up my mind that I wanted to get involved. The Sex Crimes Unit called me and asked a few questions over the phone and set up an appointment for me to come into the station and give my testimony.

A few days later Suzanne came in to work, telling my mom that she had seen Larry's picture on TV. I turned the channel to our twenty-four-hour news station and there was a mug shot of him. The newscaster explained that if any girls had been in contact with him, to call the Sex Crimes Unit. They ran the picture and hotline number all day. I called the police officer I had previously been in contact with, who told me they had arrested Larry the day before at his work. He had refused to talk. She also told me that they had been receiving calls all day from girls. At least three already knew they were infected and several more didn't know and didn't want to get tested. Only one other girl agreed to go in and give her testimony. The officer explained that no one wanted to have their name attached to this for fear of finding out they were infected or for fear of people finding out.

The day of my appointment with the police came. My mom took me down to police headquarters. We met with the two female officers heading up the case. They led us into a room with two couches, a plant, and a box of tissues on a coffee table. I could only imagine the stories that had been told in this room. They explained that they were going to videotape my interview, which would be used as evidence in their case. Larry would most likely see the tape, as evidence must be shared with both defense and prosecution. I agreed and signed the waiver. My mom was told that she had to leave the room and that I would be done in a half hour or so. Without her, I suddenly felt exposed and vulnerable. I would have to go through this alone.

I left that day and made the appointment that I never wanted to make, an appointment for an HIV test. The police told me to get one just in case. I knew that the chances of me contracting the virus were slim, but the fear was still there. The whole thing was an out-of-body experience. I could not believe I was in this position in the first place. I sat down, the doctor tied my arm, stuck me with the needle, and watched as my blood was sucked into a vial. It was my first panic attack.

I left feeling awful and went home to Mom's. I waited the next two weeks for my test results. Every night as I went to bed, I thought about it, and every morning when I woke up, I thought about it.

The day finally came to get my results. I went an hour early. I brought my friend Fadia along for moral support. The nurse went through her files. It felt like it was taking forever. She told me that I tested negative. My whole body lifted; I jumped up and hugged the nurse. The ordeal was over.

That night I couldn't help but think about Larry. He was

evil, but I still felt sorry for him to a certain degree. Two weeks of torture had ended for me; his was just beginning.

Falling asleep, safe in my bedroom that night, I thought of Marie and the other infected girls and wondered why I had been spared. Luck? Intuition?

You might never know, I told myself. *Just be happy that you're here.*

CHAPTER 23

CALIFORNIA, HERE WE COME

Joan

My job as a mother was finally winding down, and it was starting to look like a little "me time" was coming my way! Ian was
living on his own, earning his own way. Maddy had finished
high school with flying colors and was planning to travel around
Europe for six months. Thanks to her marks from Taddle Creek,
she could go almost anywhere she wanted in Canada.

Unfortunately for me, I had taken up smoking again. I
know you're supposed to lose weight when you smoke, but
I gained about ten pounds. Smoking makes me tired and, as
others have pointed out, so relaxed that I start enjoying cold
beers again. And, of course, I was no longer running like a
lunatic.

I was doing better mentally, however, thanks to a whole
lot of therapy that took me to some dark places. The therapy

had been long overdue. A lot of my old obsessive habits went by the wayside. I was going to be damned if I got myself into one more dead-end, destructive, romantic relationship with someone unsuitable. My timing for seeking this help was impeccable, as I had a fair amount of male attention. And I had a first for me: I was able to deal with it without losing my mind and turning into a blithering, needy mess.

I was restless, though, and needed a change. I was sick of the weather in Canada. Plus, with the exception of one year at the university outside of town and another in Banff, I had never lived outside of Toronto. I pictured myself jogging, watching television, and trying to quit smoking in the same town, in the same house, for the rest of my life. I was turning forty-six. If I was ever going to try something new, it would have to be now.

My business took me to Los Angeles a lot, and I'd always toyed with the fantasy of living there. Palm trees, the Pacific Ocean. Convertibles. It seemed to be just what the doctor ordered. I decided to go—to move there—and try something new.

Suzanne and I immediately began fantasizing about the "sparkling" apartment I was going to rent on the beach and how cheap it was going to be compared to my overhead in Toronto. I was still enjoying running my own company but was starting to think about doing some "good" work and giving back. I had a dream of setting up a foundation that gave out business loans to single mothers. I also wanted to quit smoking, get back into killer shape, and find a nice, laid-back man who understood me. Not too much to ask. Suzanne and I poured over one budget after another before I left. LA was going to be cheap AND life changing. Yay, Team Joan!

At the time, Maddy had been planning a trip to Europe, so I decided to coordinate my departure with hers. Ian was cool with my decision. He got particularly excited when he realized I intended to live on the beach and have the kids visit regularly. In addition, I would be back every six weeks, so we would really see a lot of each other. Maddy thought my plan was fantastic too. My God, I was brave enough to live my dreams and God bless. This was how she was starting to talk as she was getting a bit older. She was very mellow and philosophical, and even more strangely, she had taken the whole self-education thing pretty seriously and was turning into a current-affairs buff, developing some really interesting insights. I was starting to love her whole vibe.

I decided I would move to LA in January. It was September, so time was starting to close in on me. Before I left, though, I desperately needed Maddy to have her plans in place.

One night Maddy and I had a long conversation about my leaving. For the first time she admitted that her European trip just wasn't realistic, not only because she had no money or job, but also because she wasn't up for traveling around the world with a backpack and sleeping in hostels. I could have told her that, but she had convinced herself that it would be great.

"I want to go with you to LA," she said.

I smiled. My Maddy. Her idea. Just like that. We talked some more, and she said she would spend two months there and then return to Toronto to go to college. The only thing I required from her was that she have enough money saved so that she could cover her spending money while she was there. She agreed and said it didn't sound like an unreasonable request.

The more we talked, the more our fantasy flourished. We planned for endless hours how we would decorate our new apartment and what great shape we were going to be in. Even Maddy was keen on the quitting-smoking thing. She had never been a big smoker but would definitely benefit from shaking off the nasty little bastards. I loved talking to her about our plans, but found myself repeatedly clarifying that she was going to be there for only two months.

The next day she told me that she would need her own room. Hmmm. The budget Suzanne and I had constructed allowed for only a one-bedroom apartment. Suzanne and I agreed it would be worth the cost. Plus, we rationalized, if I wanted people to visit, I would need an extra bedroom.

So the budget went up by about a thousand dollars a month. Then Maddy and I talked again, and she mentioned that she wanted take a course or two while she was there. What was I supposed to say after fifteen years of extolling the virtues of a good education?

Before I knew it, we were submitting an application to Santa Monica College for a full-time student. What? How did this happen? Then she explained that there was no real point in her taking just a couple of courses. The school offered her dream program—fashion. She had always shown an incredible knack in that area, and again, who was I to get in the way of her betterment? Even though the budget was climbing, I was pretty excited about having my girl along for this once-in-a-lifetime ride.

I flew to LA later that week and found us an apartment. Even with Maddy coming along, Suzanne and I had budgeted no more than twenty-five hundred dollars per month for rent. For that amount, I could have lived like a queen in some of the one-bedroom places I was shown. Also, Maddy didn't drive (thank God), so we would need a place close to the school. These restrictions didn't help my budget. Santa Monica (which is where the college was located—thus the name) was one of the most expensive areas in LA. I had had a location farther south in mind when my plan started. There would go another grand a month. I also started worrying about Maddy's safety. I would be away on business, so we would need security. That did it. Full-time doorman. We were now up to four thousand dollars per month.

I sat on my hotel room's balcony that trip, drinking red wine and talking over the situation with Kim on the phone. I had already put a deposit on my dream apartment on the beaches of Santa Monica, but it was going to kill me financially, or at the very least, maim me badly. Somehow, between a couple of glasses of wine and an overprotective aunt, I had decided this was the right place to live while checking out our new adventure.

Suzanne, the next day, was not so enthusiastic. I told her this was what it was going to have to be. If I went broke, I went broke. I would still have the house in Toronto, which had thankfully gone up in value during a much-needed real-estate boom. We would just lease it out. We would make it work!

And so it went. Plans were made; fantasies bandied about like they were real; and Maddy, Suzanne, and I couldn't have been happier. The money was going to be a stretch, but who cared. If worse came to worst, I could collapse my retirement savings. Not something my accountant would want to hear, but I didn't care. After so many years of feeling under the gun, it was time to let go a bit. And, after all, I could run my business just as well if not better there in Tinseltown. I was convinced that I would be able to find new and better contacts for my business, and I would set the town on its ear.

When it came time for Maddy and me to leave town, friends and family got emotional—everyone except my mother, who was mighty upset and not afraid to let me know, loud and clear, that I was splitting up "her family." She was the matriarch. When I repeatedly told her we would be home a lot, she shot back with, "Maddy will meet someone and get married and so will you, and then neither of you will ever come back." I didn't picture myself getting married. I could see possibly meeting someone who would be able to travel back and forth. But that was as far as I had ever gotten even in my wildest fantasies. Maddy's romantic fantasies were not far off from mine. She wanted to meet someone and be able to travel back and forth too.

My sister, Kim, and I were devastated at being separated, but because Kim is Kim, she just smiled and said she didn't

blame me one bit for at least trying out a new life away from
Toronto. She said she knew deep down I'd be back. As heart-
wrenching as it was, she was able to put on a smile for the
occasion. As for my friends, most of them would be visiting
at some point or another, and I had a couple of friends down
there already. Plus, Maddy and I would be together, so there
wasn't going to be any room for loneliness.

When December rolled around, I had leased out my
Toronto house and was staying at Kim and Mike's, causing commotion in that house. We were making the most of
the holiday season and our last times together. By the time
Christmas hit, Maddy and I were exhausted and in desperate
need of a place to call home. At the last minute we moved up
the departure date by a couple of weeks and stole away in the
night to our new home.

We were so damned excited on the flight. I'll never forget it.
We were having a great time. We arrived in LA late at night and
hopped into our rental car. We stopped to pick up some food
and wine (so that we could toast the new place) and arrived at
our empty apartment. We had one blow-up bed, one regular
bed, and a TV, so we were fine. When Maddy saw the place,
she was blown away. Our entire living room looked out over the
ocean and mountains. We later renamed the biggest mountain
"Mount Maddy." Man, did she love that view. We had a couple
of glasses of wine and went to bed downright giddy. I was so
glad she was there with me.

The next morning was even more exciting. The mountains and the water looked just gorgeous. We thought we had

died and gone to heaven. Within a couple of hours there was a knock on the door, which we thought was strange since we didn't know anyone. The little old woman at the door, whose name was Ernestine, was our new neighbor, and she wanted to welcome us but also complain about the smell of cigarettes coming from the apartment. I figured if I was spending thousands a month on rent, I wouldn't have to worry about the neighbors, but I wanted to fit in, so I assured her that we would keep an eye on it. While she was there, she asked about what I did for a living. I hadn't learned yet that in LA you are only as good as your job. I explained that I worked in the children's entertainment industry. She gleefully explained that her "spirit guide" had told her she would be getting a big break soon, and it was going to be coming from the new tenant across the hall. It turns out she had written several children's stories and really wanted to get published. *Yeah, well, I want a pony*, I wanted to say. But instead of nipping this one in the bud, I told her I would be happy to take a look, which I did. Old Ernestine really set the tone for our stay in LA. The land of the pitch. Everywhere I went, someone was trying to drum up some business—even in the laundry room.

For the first few months I was determined to fit in, so I quit smoking, ran like a maniac, and started rebuilding my self-help library. I spent a lot of time at Oasis for Wellness, getting acupuncture and exploring New Age healing. I was so excited when one of my friends from home came to town because then I could be myself. But even with the efforts at self-improvement and wellness, I realized one day that I felt old in a young town. Maddy, on the other hand, was having the time of her life. She was doing extremely well in school and generally finding her groove. She loved going to the clubs with her new friend Terra, who was in charge of the leasing office in our apartment complex. She was becoming like family to both of us. I hated when Maddy went out, though. LA was a far cry from Toronto in terms of violence. It boasted a well-developed underbelly, and I worried more than ever about her. I tried not to obsess over her safety—to breathe—and let go. She was older now, I told myself, and she was even on the dean's list.

After a few months of jogging and schmoozing and pitching, I got tired of trying to be perfect all the time and realized I really wasn't meant to be in LA. I hated living in an apartment and being checked out every time I got on the elevator. The residents weren't checking me out with interest—but with horror. I was one of the only forty-six-year-old women who had the nerve to wander around without plastic surgery or, at the very least, some Botox. I'm not against these things but am just too scared to start messing with myself. With my luck, my face would collapse or something. I was a constant reminder to the locals of what they would look like if they hadn't nipped and tucked. Nobody wanted that reminder, so no one wanted to hang with me. *I am a woman, not a monster*, I wanted to scream. The place wasn't working for me. I was bored and lonely—two feelings I don't have often.

There was one problem with going home—Maddy had settled in and was doing wonderfully. I didn't know how I was going to make it, but I knew I had to hang in there for Maddy's sake. She was flourishing, and just because LA wasn't working for me, I didn't have the right to rain on her parade. *I can do this*, I told myself. *Heck, at least it's sunny.*

CHAPTER 24

A ROOM WITH A VIEW

Maddy

After I graduated from Taddle Creek in the spring, my mom told me she was moving to California. I was planning on moving to London the next winter, and Ian was on his own, so I thought the move would be a great way for her to start her new life as a single, independent woman. We talked for hours about what her new life would be like in Los Angeles. I told her that I would fly back from Europe to help her move and get settled. We planned and planned—from where she would live to what our reunions would be like. Both of us needed a change.

There was just one problem. When I graduated with honors from Taddle Creek, I couldn't get a job, and I desperately needed to save money for London. I was determined to find work and not have yet another one of my plans fall through.

By the time fall rolled around, I started losing steam and

doubting myself. I pretended to hit the pavement day after day, claiming that looking for a job was like a job in itself. I came up with every excuse in the book. I was underqualified, I was overqualified, there were no jobs out there. My mom got fed up. She would kick me out of the house every day at nine and not permit me to come back until six in the evening. Finally I called in a favor from my friend Chris and got a job at the butcher shop where she worked. I started the next day.

The butcher shop was a high-quality meat place in the heart of the gay district in Toronto. The pay was good but the hours were long. I started at eight in the morning and finished at seven in the evening. My duties were to organize the food in the morning, serve customers all day, and clean the shop at the end of the day. I had trouble remembering all of the prices, which frustrated my coworkers. I was also not skilled at wrapping the meat in the paper but gave it my best shot. I would often confuse my orders, and the customers were not always understanding. But the real problem that I had there was in accepting how seniority worked. I would be busy doing something, and my coworkers, who had the exact same position at the shop that I had, would ask me to go to the back and get whatever. If I wasn't busy and they were, I could understand putting me to use, but that wasn't the case. They had two legs and two hands, so why in the hell should I drop everything to do their work? I would tell them that I was busy and they would have to do it. They did not take kindly to my lack of respect for the longtime employees.

Three weeks into my new job, the boss asked to talk to

me. It was the end of my shift and I was exhausted. He pulled me aside and told me that he had learned that I was planning on moving to London in two months. I told him that, yes, that was true, and then he told me I was fired. He said that he needed someone on a more permanent basis and that it wasn't going to work. I asked if I should stay on until they found someone else. When he said no, I shouldn't come back, I had a sneaking suspicion that I was fired for other reasons. Anyone who has gotten fired knows that it's awkward. I told my mom that night what had happened, and she told me that I'd better find a new job quickly because she wasn't going to California until I was settled.

I didn't look for another job. Instead, I hung out with my friends and partied. My mom finally got fed up with me and decided to take serious action. This time she didn't just kick me out of her house, but took it a step further and kicked me out of the province. She told me that she couldn't organize a move and worry about me getting a job, so I would be on the next plane out to Halifax, Nova Scotia, to live with my dad. She thought that he might have better luck making me get a job. While I had been sleeping away from home the night before, she booked me a ticket for two days from then. I was impressed. She knew how to get me where it hurt. I had underestimated her, and she was now winning.

The night before I left for Halifax, I partied with two of my best girlfriends, Molly and Tina. Everything was fine until it was time for me to go home. I realized that I might never see them again. We cried. I think the alcohol had something to do with it. I then made up my mind that in no way would I board that plane to Halifax, come hell or high water. I went back to my mom's house. I marched right up to her, yelling about how I was not going to Halifax. She told me to call my father about this. I wasn't thinking clearly and did just as she told me to. I dialed his number and woke my stepmom. I hadn't realized that it was three in the morning there. Oops. I told her to put my dad on. He sounded worried, as any parent would be getting a call in the middle of the night. I yelled that I hated him and that I didn't want to go to his house because I would be miserable. He told me that he didn't know where all of this anger was coming from and asked if I had been drinking. This angered me even further. He said that he didn't want his house to be a place where I go to be punished and that if I didn't want to come, I didn't have to. I told my mom this. She said that I did, in fact, have to. I called him back and told him that I would see him later that day.

I woke up in the morning with one badass hangover. My mom drove me to the airport. When we approached the check-in lady, she looked at me like I had the face of a monster. My eyes were puffy from crying. I have never been a pretty crier; my face gets all scrunched up and my blood vessels pop. I was leaning on the desk, weak from my activities of the night before. When my ticket was organized and I was gearing up to leave my mom, the woman asked if I needed assistance to my gate. The nerve! My mom and I had a good chuckle about that as we said our good-byes. She and I were now getting along, and she was sad that I had to go. I reminded her that it was her fault I was leaving in the first place but that I would see her in six weeks. As I walked away, she yelled after me, "You better get a job." My mom is not a quitter.

I was nervous about seeing my dad. I had gone off on him when he really hadn't deserved it. When I arrived in Halifax, I apologized and told him that I was actually happy to see him and to be there. I did even less in Halifax than I had done in Toronto. Every day I would wake up around noon, wander downstairs, then drink tea and smoke cigarettes until about five when my dad would come home. Just before he was due to arrive, I would get dressed so that I looked like I had been busy. He would ask how my job search was going, and I would just say "slow."

I decided that while in Halifax, I would try and get my driver's license. I had had my learner's permit for over a year but hadn't tried to get my actual license. I didn't see the need to have a license in Toronto since I took the subway and taxis. It may have also had something to do with the fact that my mom wouldn't let me drive with her in the car. We attempted it once, but she just ended up yelling at me to stay farther away from parked cars. We gave up after five minutes. In her defense, I am a bad driver. I have a heavy foot and no sense of distance. My dad took it upon himself to instruct me. Becky, my stepmother, arranged for me to take professional lessons, as well. I took two lessons and skipped the other two. The driving instructor told me that in no way was I ready to actually take my test, but I thought that he was trying to squeeze more money out of my dad and Becky. I got ready for my test and told all of my friends back home to be prepared, because I was going to return licensed. I got all dolled up in my prettiest outfit and did my hair and makeup. I figured that the instructor might overlook a few mistakes if he liked how I looked. Becky and I waited for my instructor at the Department of Motor Vehicles. I was shocked and disappointed when a heavyset, stone-faced woman walked out. She looked me up and down; I knew I was in trouble.

The test started out fine. It wasn't until I had to make a left-hand turn at a light that things went from good to bad. I decided to proceed, then got stuck in the middle of the intersection while waiting for the oncoming traffic to clear. The light quickly went from green to yellow to red. I gunned it. All of a sudden a car came out of nowhere and swerved in front of me. I slammed on the breaks. "Shit!!" As I proceeded, I asked the woman if I had failed. She looked at me and shook her head in disbelief at my stupidity. I drove back to the dealership after not being able to parallel park or even pull up to a curb. As she got out of the car, she turned to me and said, "I hope for the sake of all other drivers that you never get your license."

That night I had a dream I was driving with my mom down Sunset Boulevard. We had a convertible and my driving skills were perfect. I felt happy and in control. I woke up the next morning with a plan. I started researching colleges in California. At Taddle Creek I had discovered fashion and design and had never been more motivated or interested in something in my life. I found a program in design at Santa

Monica College that seemed perfect for me. Determined to make it happen, I called my mom, discussed my options, and flew back to Toronto the next day.

Once back in Toronto, my mom and I started planning our move together. Suzanne got us both visas, a bigger apartment, and before I knew it, my dream was becoming a reality.

Before heading west, our good-bye festivities started. I didn't see the need to spend the whole time with my friends since it was just before Christmas and I was not scheduled to leave until after New Year's. That schedule changed quickly, however, when my mom rescheduled our plans. She wanted to leave right after Christmas. I was upset and disappointed because I wanted to ring in the new year with my friends. *Grow up*, I told myself.

My mom and I left on December 26 for the airport and took off for our greatest adventure ever. When we got to Los Angeles, it was dark. Our new apartment was gorgeous. The complex was called "The Shores." It was a luxury high-rise. My mom gave me a brief tour of the grounds, showing me the pool, the store, and the gym. I loved it all. The next day she woke me up early so I could look at the view. I turned my head away from the wall and saw the most beautiful view from my bed—the ocean, the mountains, and palm trees! I thought that I had died and gone to heaven. We spent the first four days organizing our apartment. Later in the week, New Year's rolled around. I spent the night putting together IKEA furniture. The phone rang right as twelve hit. Chris was calling from a party. I missed home for a moment, but after I got off the phone, I went to my balcony, which overlooked the ocean. I sat there staring at a Ferris wheel lit up on the pier in the distance, thinking that this move would be the best thing that ever happened to me.

I met Terra the following week at the leasing office, located in the building. I felt suddenly uncomfortable for some reason—like the new kid in school—but told myself that if I wanted to make friends there was no room for being awkward. Terra and I became fast friends. Through her, I made more friends and even met the first guy I would date in LA. Everything was good. I was starting school, and I had a female friend and a boyfriend. I found it easy to adjust. When school started, I was nervous but I adjusted to that easily, as well.

I loved my new life and missed nothing about Toronto. My mom didn't seem to be having as good a time as I was though. She often said how much she missed home. I couldn't understand why. Over the next eight months I enjoyed the good life. I lost a bunch of weight and had a super tan. Only one of my friends from Toronto came to visit me, even though all of them had promised that they would. Kate was the only person who actually managed to get off her ass and come. She was impressed with the new me. I felt like a million bucks. I fantasized that she would return to Canada, telling tales of my new Hollywood life.

After Kate left, I started thinking constantly about my old friends and my life back in Toronto. I was twenty years old and fitting in here; why was I looking back? Some days I would be trying to focus on a homework assignment, and I would suddenly get dizzy and nervous. The room would start spinning, and I would have to stop what I was doing and try to regain control. I tried shaking it off and telling myself that I was just tired or overworked, but something was different. Or rather, something wasn't right.

Chapter 25

911

Joan

Just another morning in LA. I was on day two of quitting smoking, and I was feeling strong. I was about to go for a run on the beach and was trying to convince myself that I loved it here when the phone rang. It was Maddy's friend Terra screaming, "Maddy is on the floor unconscious! She has blood coming out of her mouth!"

I immediately went into autopilot. I needed to get to Maddy right away. I dropped the phone and managed to make it to Terra's apartment in record time. Time had never moved so slowly—I wanted to scream in the elevator. I gunned the car out of the underground parking lot at about eighty miles an hour. Luckily, I was moving against the rush hour traffic, but that didn't stop me from leaning on the horn at various times. The torturous ten minutes were spent alternately screaming and crying on the phone to my sister, Kim, back in Toronto, and then calmly talking to Terra and the paramedics, who were with Maddy at Terra's apartment. *Oh my God*, I thought, *what if this is it?* I was losing my baby girl to some fatal condition. I was shaking like a leaf and just wanted to get to her before it was too late.

I pulled into the parking lot of Terra's building right behind an ambulance with its back doors open. Terra was in her pajamas, and a couple of paramedics were waiting for me. I bolted out of my car and made a beeline for them. When I saw my little girl lying on the stretcher, my heart broke into a million pieces. I have never loved someone so much or been so terrified. I climbed into the ambulance and answered the paramedics' questions as best I could while stroking Maddy's head and squeezing her hand, telling her everything was going to be all right. I didn't believe one word coming out of my mouth. She didn't know the day of the week and couldn't remember where she was. But she was speaking. At least she was speaking.

Off we went for the torturous ten-minute ride to the hospital. Maddy was completely disoriented. But her eyes started looking a little more alive by the time we got to the emergency room. We were able to get her settled in quickly and within an hour or so, she was pretty much back to her old self again—kind of. The battery of tests was well under way, and after about an hour, we started getting some encouraging results. My most deep-seated fears were being calmed—no leukemia, no brain tumor, no abnormalities in her blood work. The terror was lifting, and it was time to have a good cry by myself in the parking lot, out of her sight. The doctor on call decided that she had probably had a seizure.

Maddy has never been a big drug user. As she grew older, pot made her feel anxious, even though she was an advocate for its legalization, and coke and Ecstasy were things she told me she had tried but didn't like. She had explained to me on different occasions that being up all night and greeting the sun was too bleak (given that statement, I gathered that she had dabbled), so I had never spent much time worrying about her becoming a drug addict. Thank God, I told myself, I didn't need to worry about that. Alcohol, on the other hand, Maddy enjoyed. Like mother like daughter. I have always enjoyed a good party and am still trying to find an alternative for alcohol that offers so much in such little time. I come from drinkers and I'm a drinker, so it would follow that my kids would be drawn to it too.

Sitting at the hospital, my thoughts started to spin. As far as I could tell, Maddy had gotten herself run down from late nights, crappy food, and cocktails. I realized that I was in a blissful state of denial about Maddy's lifestyle while she was in Montreal. I was so hell-bent to make this move work for ME that I had convinced myself that everything and everybody around me would be okay. Since this was supposed to have been the Year of Joan, I craved some time away from all the worries that normally plagued me as a mother. I had started taking Paxil to find the calmer, less fretful self lurking deep within. I was trying to adjust to LA and find a new serene me. And, of course, I had quit smoking.

My mind flashed back to just two months before. Maddy had started complaining that she missed her friends back home, so I agreed to let her go back for a visit and get a job for the summer. She said she didn't know what was wrong with her—that she felt kind of shaky and sad. Thinking that she was homesick, I booked her a ticket to Montreal, where she and her friends were planning a reunion. Five weeks later I got a call from Maddy in Montreal. She was sobbing into the phone, telling me she was completely out of control and totally humiliated. The poor girl was terrified. She said she was having a panic attack. It was time for Momma to take her head out of her ass and look alive. I worked the phone lines and got her to Kim's in Toronto within twenty-four hours. Maddy stayed there long enough to visit a doctor, who said she was fine, and then was on a plane back to LA within a day.

When I picked her up at the airport, I saw that she had become tiny. Maddy had never been little—she was always strong and voluptuous. Now her chest was flat, her thickish legs were skinny, and the span of her back was about as wide as my thigh. Was she going for heroin chic? I kid you not, I was convinced that the bleeding gums, the bruising, and her over-all shakiness could be cured with some good old-fashioned Momma love, good food, and megadoses of vitamins. The doctor in Toronto had said she was fine but possibly anemic. She had been away for just more than a month, but from where I was sitting, her affliction looked more like scurvy. I had access to citrus, being in California, so hell, we would just get to work on healing her. But now I realized, as I was sitting in the emergency room, things had gotten worse, and vitamin C wasn't going to cut it.

Later that night when we got home from the hospital, I held her as she fell asleep. The doctors still didn't know what was wrong with her.

Over the next month she gained much of the weight back and was beginning to act like the old Maddy. Even though she was still on shaky ground, she went out. She kept insisting she was fine and not partaking in any drug activity.

Once school was back in session, two weeks later, she began showing signs of anxiety again. She was having trouble getting out of the apartment and having particular difficulty with the hallway in the building. The lights were making her feel sketchy, she said. Let's face facts—nobody should struggle with a hallway. Enough of this, I said. It was time to get her to another doctor. From what I could tell by doing research on the Internet, many of her symptoms pointed to a potential panic disorder. We were in Southern California, land of dysfunction, so surely somebody could figure this out for us.

Enter Dr. FeelGood, who was recommended by some friends of mine in Tinseltown. He was both a psychiatrist and a neurologist, which sounded impressive. When we got to his office, we were handed a bunch of forms held together by a clipboard with the Prozac logo all over it. It was then that I noticed that the coffee mugs, the water cooler, the pens—pretty much everything in his office—carried an advertisement for some type of name-brand antidepressant or antianxiety drug. I hadn't realized that the medical community was so heavily into licensed merchandise (an area I knew from the children's business). It's one thing to have Elmo all over a pair of slippers but another to be reading about the virtues of Prozac while sipping a cup of coffee—oh California!

I wasn't allowed in with Maddy for her consultation (which I had to pay cash for, being a foreigner and having messed up my health-coverage situation), but she came out after forty-five minutes looking considerably more chipper and armed with meds and prescriptions. We were making headway. When Maddy explained that the doctor had told her she had a panic disorder, and that the medications prescribed would take care of it, I was all too happy to embrace the diagnosis. We talked on the drive back to Santa Monica about what had been discussed, and we both became convinced that the meds were the answer.

After about three or four weeks of Maddy taking the meds, which included an antidepressant and an anticonvulsant (high dosages, we later found out), her mood was becoming flatter and her energy level was ridiculously low. We were trapped together in a two-bedroom apartment with nowhere to go. Her schoolwork started slipping early in the term. Maddy would lie on my bed watching daytime television while I worked in the dining room. I hadn't felt so trapped, pissed off, or worried about her since her teen years. But we were hopeful from this new doctor's diagnosis, so we were going to see it through.

Normal activities like going to a restaurant for lunch became interrupted by Maddy's immediate and desperate need to get back home. A walk to the beach could end in tears of confusion and despair. Maddy was desperate to resume a normal life without the terror of the panic attacks. We were becoming paralyzed by the situation—everything felt overwhelming. We were in a strange land with a strange thing going down, trying to ride it out. We took the smallest victories as signs of progress, kidding ourselves into believing that everything was going to be fine.

Maddy did go out once in a while with Terra and a couple of other friends she had met at school. She told me she was drinking only moderately, and I believed her. On the odd evening she would go out, I was relieved to have some time to myself to do nothing more than just stare at the TV and try to recuperate from the intensity that had come to define our life.

When Terra found herself a new apartment and asked Maddy to help her on moving day, it seemed like a perfectly reasonable way for two young girls to spend a day. Maddy, a couple of nights before the moving day, had stayed out late partying. The next day she looked run down and had all kinds of bruises on her legs. When she arrived home from Montreal with bruises, we had concluded they were due to low iron. But they were back. Why were they showing up again? Still, I allowed her to help Terra move and told her to call me if they needed any help.

On the phone with Suzanne outside the emergency room, it became apparent that the health coverage that I thought was in place was not. Excellent. In between visits to Maddy in the emergency room, I was crying on the phone to Suzanne, instructing her to pull out all the money we had in the business account. It wasn't much since LA was costing me a fortune. Kim, Ian, and my mom were all on the phone with me at various points, helping me keep it together.

By the time Maddy got discharged from the hospital, she was looking tired but otherwise well. Her spirit and sense of humor were surfacing nicely. We actually started laughing on the way home. Finding ourselves in this hard-core West LA emergency room filled with druggies and crazies seemed funny to us.

The next day we went back to her neurologist's office. The consultation was going to cost some more money, so I dropped Maddy off and headed to the ATM. It was about two hundred degrees outside and I felt like I was going to pass out. The shock was starting to wear off, which left me feeling sick and tired. But the show must go on, so I got the cash and headed back to the doctor's office.

The doctor came into the exam room. She was probably only four foot eight, but she had a presence. She got right down to it and grilled Maddy about what she had been up to in terms of partying, sleeping, eating—the whole thing. I felt like she had a bright light shining in Maddy's face, but she was getting some answers. It turned out that Maddy had not been limiting her alcohol intake to one or two drinks on her nights out. When the doctor heard about her experience in Montreal, she quickly concluded that Maddy had had a seizure that morning. Maddy would have to cut out alcohol, caffeine, and certainly drugs. Maddy took it in stride, asking the question any of us would: "How long should I avoid this stuff?" When she heard the answer, the floor dropped out from under both of us. The doctor told her it would have to be "forever." The tyke's face registered a combination of horror, disbelief, heartbreak, and fury. It was not great news for Maddy, but it was excellent news for me.

The doctor instructed Maddy to stop taking the other medications over the course of the next couple of days and start a new anticonvulsant script. The new treatment seemed straightforward, but we still didn't know what had triggered the seizure. The bottom line, however, was clear—no partying anymore, forever. During a subsequent conversation between Maddy and the doctor a week or so later, it came out that she had been doing cocaine and Ecstasy while in Montreal. As far as the doctor was concerned, the drugs explained it all. In her opinion, Maddy was lucky to be alive.

It was time to pull the plug on our LA adventure. My ex-boyfriend Alex was kind enough to come in and watch Maddy for a couple of days while I went to Canada. I bought an old farmhouse in a small town north of Toronto, just ten minutes from Kim. I felt like Maddy's hero, Dorothy, who had learned there was no place like home. Maddy was upset by my decision but knew it was the right one. Within six weeks Maddy was on a plane home, and I was there shortly after. Terra's boyfriend had agreed to drive a U-Haul carrying all of our stuff home for me.

So there we were, trying to find a little peace and quiet and settle into our new "Reba McEntire" dream home in the country. Maddy was doing well and had been taken off all medication. The medical conclusion that had been reached was that she had set off the panic attacks by using drugs during the summer, and that the medication Dr. FeelGood had prescribed had been all wrong and triggered the actual seizure.

Christmas season arrived, along with all of Maddy's friends from various locations. It was time to party, but not for Maddy. She kept assuring me that I didn't need to worry about her. Two or three weeks later and a whole pile of overnights downtown, Maddy was not doing so well anymore. She told me she was using restraint and having a beer or two along the way. My gut told me something completely different but what was I supposed to do—she had just turned twenty-one and was an adult who had to make her own decisions.

Just after the holidays (post–New Year's Eve), Maddy was at the Reba house along with my gay painter/decorator and Suzanne and her one-year-old baby. We were having an idyllic morning. I was feeling particularly blissed out having my people around me and decorating my new home. Maddy had slept in late, as was her habit, and then came downstairs to have a cup of tea. She had been with me for five days. She hadn't had any alcohol, had been eating good food, and was taking lots of vitamins. Maddy was in the kitchen using the laptop, and within two seconds of me leaving the kitchen, she took a huge fall onto the floor. I ran in and there she was writhing on the floor, eyes rolling back in her head, mouth foaming, and skin turning blue. I yelled to the others to call an ambulance. I got down on the floor and rode it out with her. The seizure lasted about ninety seconds and then she went limp.

Her seizure was the most terrifying sight ever. I thought she was going to die; her face was blue. Holding her in my arms on the kitchen floor, I felt, for the first time in my life, completely powerless. *What am I going to do? How can I help and protect this child, my little girl?*

It's like grabbing at water, I suddenly realized. There were no words to express the depth of my love or my pain or my frustration. I couldn't predict or plan or ensure her well-being.

As I rocked her back and forth and waited for yet another ambulance to arrive, I whispered in her ear all I could think to offer her: "It's okay, I'm here."

When we got into the emergency room, the doctors took a look at her right away and concluded that indeed this was a seizure that was more than likely caused by drugs and alcohol. Yes, it's true. Maddy had, as it turned out, done cocaine and drank huge amounts over the holidays. What was it going to take to get this kid to get it together?

Maddy had now been told by four or five doctors not to drink or do drugs. I couldn't see where the confusion was for her. I wanted to shake her and scream, *Get it together*, but all I could muster was a series of hugs and kisses as she cried in my arms. We would get through this together, I kept saying. We would forge ahead and both live sober. At this point I would have cut off my right arm for her health, so maybe just maybe I could take a look at myself and stop drinking as well. Would it kill me? It might if this stress level stuck around.

CHAPTER 26

DÉJÀ VU

Maddy
When I was a child, I was always pretty healthy. The only thing that I really struggled with were my random bouts of "déjà vu." For most people this is a feeling of reliving an experience that you could swear you've been in before. This feeling is usually followed with a comment such as, "I could have sworn I have done this exact thing before."

This is not how déjà vu hit me. I would be doing some simple thing like organizing what I would bring to show-and-tell when I would be overcome with dizziness and an extreme case of nausea. My mom understood what had to be done. Every time I would stagger up to her, my little face all white and soggy, telling her I was "having déjà vu," she would put me to bed for the day and carry on. Everyone but my mom tried to contradict what it was that I was feeling, but I knew exactly what I was talking about. Not for one second did she second-guess my choice of words. It was simply déjà vu and that's all there was to it. One day the déjà vu stopped. I never had that feeling again, at least not strong enough to make me feel as though I was going to pass out. I became just like the masses and used the term to mean enjoying the rerun of a situation. Little did we know that déjà vu in the sense I had experienced it is a common precursor to epilepsy.

One time my brother had to spend three weeks in the hospital, and I saw all of the candy and concern that he got. I wanted in on that action. When I was about twelve, I had convinced myself that I had breast cancer. I didn't have breasts but felt these two little bumps, one under each nipple. For two weeks I was alone with my cancer, too embarrassed to tell my mom. Eventually I got up the nerve. The anxiety was too much to deal with on my own. I sat her down and said, "I'm sorry to have to tell you this, but I have breast cancer and it's in both of my boobs." I felt bad for my mom because, after all, no parent wants to outlive his or her child. My mom gave me a look that said, *You poor idiot*. She told me that I didn't have breast cancer, but rather, was starting to develop actual boobs. Words cannot explain the humiliation I felt. Then she talked to me about becoming a woman and commented on how she had noticed my recently acquired hips. She suggested we go shopping for a bra. I made a promise to myself that day—I would never go to her with a chronic illness again.

I survived my teen years without contracting a disease, which I had always thought was a minor miracle. Sure, there were times when I was certain that I had a brain tumor. At one point I thought I might have schizophrenia. The doctor always assured me that I was healthy both physically and mentally. It wasn't until my summer in Montreal that my premonition of poor health came to pass. I was twenty and had just spent the last six months living the dream in Los Angeles with my mom. I missed my friends and wanted to visit them. Montreal is a little taste of Europe, but with the party scene Canada is known for. I was planning on staying for a few weeks. I had lost that extra ten pounds and was enjoying the bond with my girlies that I had been missing for the previous six months. We ran the city.

It wasn't until my mom's good friend from New York came to town to take me to dinner that I felt the pain that results from a few weeks of poor living. Dinner was to be my break from bad food but turned out to be the beginning of a downward spiral. I went to her friend's hotel with a friend for a predinner drink. The switch from no-name vodka to Belvedere was greatly appreciated. The joint I smoked outside after that was where I went wrong. I had quit smoking weed but figured, what the hell, it's a special occasion. I was fine until about ten minutes after I smoked the joint. I lost it. I was tripping out like never before. I didn't want anyone to know my condition, so I locked myself in the bathroom, knelt down on the floor with my elbows on the sink counter and my hands over my face, and quietly talked myself down. "Honestly, don't do this. Now, get your fucking shit together; you're embarrassing yourself." After urging myself to leave the bathroom, I went back into the lounge and helped myself to another drink. I had it under control, so we went to dinner. Midway through a bite of my fabulous pasta dish, I broke down again. I sat back in my chair and tripped. I had no choice but to tell my dinner dates what was going on. They suggested I get some rest.

I walked into my friend Kate's apartment where I was staying and cried myself to sleep. From that day on I would never feel normal again. I had entered a new reality somewhere between the joint and the pasta. Never before did I feel so lonely. The next day I called my mom. I couldn't make long-distance calls from the apartment, so I forced myself to go to the hotel across the street to make a collect call. I instructed my mom to call the apartment in five minutes. She knew something was up. The second I picked up that long-distance call, I started crying. I didn't know what was happening to me. The worst thing about making the call was hearing her disappointment. This was my fault, resulting from poor decision-making. I was embarrassed about not being able to look after myself at the age of twenty. Arrangements were made for me to return to my mom in California. I was still a child who, at the end of the day, needed her mommy. I was not the grown-up that I thought I was when I arrived in Montreal.

When I got to California, my mom was shocked to see how much weight I had lost. It was the first time that she and I both noticed what I actually looked like. I was wasting away, which for me is very hard. My skin was an odd shade of gray, I had bruises all over my legs (I'm talking *all over*), and my gums were bleeding from lack of nutrition. It was as though I had scurvy, which shouldn't happen unless you're a sailor anytime before the nineteenth century. It was not an acceptable condition to be in for a twenty-year-old, upper-middle-class girl in one of the most progressive countries.

For a while I didn't have any more episodes like the one in Montreal. But that was short lived. I started school again and was eager to redeem myself with some good marks. About a month into my regular life, the panic episodes started again. This time they arrived almost every day. After a week of not being able to leave the apartment for fear of having this happen in public, my mom got the name of a highly recommended neurologist/psychiatrist who would take me right away. It was quite an experience going into the doctor's office. Everything from his clipboard to his pens to his mugs had some sort of drug name on it, from Ambien to Prozac. This guy was seriously sponsored. I took it as a good sign. After all, sponsors are looking for good people to carry their name. This guy had access to the top contenders when it came to drugs. I sat in the chair adjacent to him and answered his questions. I described how it felt to have one of these episodes. "It's as if I all of a sudden have this overwhelming feeling that turns into tunnel vision and an inability to hear properly, kind of like someone has put his hands over my ears. Basically, I'm tripping." He marked all of this down on his pad of paper, responding with an annoying, "Uh-huh." By the end of my half-hour session, I was diagnosed with panic disorder and prescribed both an antidepressant and an antianxiety drug. I felt okay about all of this if it would give me the ability to leave the apartment. In high school I had known a couple of people who had panic attacks, and they seemed to have turned out fine. Quick fixes are just that, quick.

The medication didn't help me return to my old reality, but rather it put me in a numb state. It was an improvement on feeling like the world was caving in on me. But neither feeling is ideal. I didn't notice the effect of the antidepressant as much as that of the antianxiety medication. I took one pill a day and was instructed to take another if I felt the onset of an attack. I was told that I could take as many as four a day. Whenever I did take an extra one, however, I would be so wiped out that I would sleep for twelve hours. This kept me from going to school on many occasions. I was falling more and more behind in my classes and had to weather the embarrassment of handing my teachers countless doctor's notes. It was that look of pity on their faces that really got to me, as if they didn't want to bother me in fear of me snapping. I wasn't crazy, at least I hoped not. I didn't really know what I was anymore.

When I got used to the drugs, I tried to get back to my normal activities, like going out. I had permission from my doctor to drink, but he told me to cut down on my drinking by half. I knew that didn't mean half of a twenty-six-ounce bottle of vodka. I just wanted to get back to being who I was prior to my breakdown. One morning I was hungover but kept my commitment to help my very good friend Terra move into her new place. We worked all day moving boxes and putting together her new furniture. We both felt like shit but moved mechanically through the day. Even the guy I liked came and helped, which kept me going.

Later that night I stood on Terra's balcony looking out over the busy Los Angeles street, with the warm October air against me (I had learned in class that as a result of the Santa Ana winds, it was the hottest time of the year by the beach). What happened next is a little fuzzy, but from what I can remember, I butted my cigarette and then nothing. I have no idea what happened. I woke up on Terra's bed. She was rubbing my arm and looked concerned. I had an odd sense of calm; my body was relaxed to the point of not feeling. She started asking me questions.

"Do you remember what happened, sweetie?"

My voice was soft and shaky. "Uhh . . . what?"

The paramedics had come through the door with Terra. This was really confusing but my mind was in such an altered state that I asked no questions. They checked my vital signs and asked me some questions. "What day of the week is it, Maddy?"

"Uh, Tuesday." It was a Thursday.

"Who is the president?"

I had no answer for this one, so I ignored the question all together. It's weird not knowing anything. It didn't scare me because I didn't know what fear was at that point. I knew absolutely nothing; none of it made sense. It was as though I didn't exist. They put me on the stretcher and pushed me down the hall, brought me down the elevator, and put me into the ambulance. By this time I was coming to and realized that being on a stretcher wasn't a good thing. The moment I saw my mom run up to me, I started crying and so did she. I have never seen her look so little. She herself looked like a child who needed someone to protect her. I wasn't able to do that. Terra was crying in the parking lot and was told to follow us in my mom's car to the hospital. I asked my mom the question that needed to be asked. "Am I going to die?" She answered no, but there was doubt on her face. She couldn't know what was going to happen. But hearing those words comforted me like a warm blanket.

The paramedic again asked me the questions that were previously administered. The question of what day it was, I once again answered wrong. But when asked who the president was, I answered with certainty. "Fucking Bush." This answer seemed to relieve them. We got to the hospital where they hooked me up to an IV and the vital-signs monitor. Then the nurse gave me the gown. I was panic-stricken. I had no underwear on. This worried me more than anything. I guess this is why they say always wear nice underwear when leaving the house. I was so embarrassed. I had to ask for two gowns, one to cover my bum and the other for the front. When they said that I would probably have to stay the night, I instructed my mom to get me underwear. Soon after, the doctor asked me point-blank if I had done any drugs. I don't know why, but I can't lie to doctors, so I told him that, yes, I had done cocaine and Ecstasy. That's when they stopped looking at me as a victim and started looking at me as a "drug user." I may have exercised poor judgment but that didn't automatically make me a drug addict.

I didn't have to stay the night at the hospital because they found nothing wrong with me. My blood work came out clear, as did my CT scan. They set me up with a new neurologist, who I went to see straight from the ER. Her office was different from my original neurologist's. It was much more understated and cheaply furnished. There must be a reason why some doctors are more expensive than others. It's like buying brand-name toilet paper as opposed to saving that dollar. Saving the dollar feels good at the time, but your bum will pay the price in the end. The moment I met Dr. H, I knew we wouldn't see eye to eye on anything.

Like all the others, she wrote down the story of how I had ended up there and asked the question regarding illegal drugs. I was comfortable saying yes because my mom already knew. I told her how much I drank. She told me that I had had a seizure (this was speculation; there were no tests declaring that to be the case), and if I ever had another sip of alcohol, I would die, not to even mention the ramifications of taking drugs. I had no problem with drugs being eliminated from my world. I had already decided not to dabble anymore. But never drink again? That was extreme. As soon as she said that, my face went from soft to hard. I couldn't have given that woman a dirtier look. My mom loved the idea of me never drinking again. What parent wouldn't? Her worrying would be cut down by at least 75 percent.

The doctor prescribed me antiseizure medication and took me off of my antidepressant and antianxiety medication. She also suggested that perhaps I go to rehab. That's were she crossed the line. Until that point, I was following what she was saying: I may have thought it was over the top, but who was I to question her. It was so typical of a Southern California doctor. I admit to experimenting, and she is prepared to instruct my already worried mother to send me to the Betty Ford Center for treatment. To my surprise, my mom defended me. She knew me well enough to know that the situation had scared me enough to never want to do drugs again.

After that long and stressful day, I was at a loss as to where I would go from there. No definite answers had been given to explain what happened to me that day. Instead, I was in for a long battery of testing. My mom was exhausted. Even so, she checked on me throughout the night to make sure I didn't convulse in my sleep. The experience was probably harder on the people around me than it was for me. As time dragged on, I grew so scared of having a seizure that I didn't leave the apartment for a full three weeks. Coming off the antidepressant proved to be the hardest. I wasn't depressed before I was on them but surely was after they left my system. I also become judgmental as a sober person. I gave looks when someone opened their fifth beer, rolled my eyes when someone slurred a word, and asked for music to be turned down. Telling myself that I was better than everyone else was the only way that I could deal with the envy.

After the first month of dealing with a potential chronic illness, I convinced myself that the ordeal was nothing more than an isolated incident. The doctor had taken me off the antiseizure medication, and I was feeling a lot better. I had stopped going to school and was way too far behind to even try and catch up, as it was already midsemester (around late October). On the one-month anniversary of my sobriety, I made the poor decision to start drinking again. I was in denial regarding my boundaries. I refused to be sober at twenty. My mom was shocked. She wondered how someone could care so little about her health. After I continued to cross the line, she decided to move us back to Canada. I was less than pleased but had no choice. As I boarded the plane, I kept telling myself the same thing: I couldn't afford a seizure in Canada. But I went straight from the airport to Chris's house, dropped my bags, and we headed to the bar.

Just like that, I was right back in my party mind-set. At the beginning of December I became reacquainted with a guy I had known in high school, and we started a Christmas romance. We partied hard together. One night I was particularly drunk and decided that doing a line of coke or two wouldn't be the worst thing in the world. The next three weeks were a downward spiral. I stayed at the guy's house most of the time and vacillated between being drunk and being hungover. By the time New Year's had come and gone, so had he.

I returned to my mom's and took a five-day break. When the weekend arrived, I got ready to go back to the city. My mom, Suzanne, and Alan (my mom's painter) were at the house that morning. I remember I was drinking a cup of tea and everything was fine until I felt this overwhelming pain in my back. I let my body go with it. I bent back and lost control. I don't remember anything beyond that, but I woke up on a stretcher once again and heard my mom begging the paramedics to tell her what was wrong with me.

This was strike two. I was in the hospital all day getting

tested for various illnesses. Test after test came back clear. I lay there knowing exactly what was wrong. When asked if I had been drinking, I told them yes, I had. Then the question I feared the most came along—had I been doing any drugs? I looked at my mom, then down at my chest.

Here it was: another chance to lie, to manipulate, to cover my ass. Another Maddy moment. Another chance to hide.

Enough. I can't do this anymore. Enough is enough.

"Yes," I said. "I've been using cocaine."

JOAN'S EPILOGUE

I sometimes think back to the years when Maddy was younger, when she always had an excuse, when she would lie to me, and, I swear to God, please don't judge me, a part of me thinks that life was easier back then.

It's been one year since we moved back home from Tinseltown. Maddy lives with a girlfriend, has a job and a great new boyfriend (at least for now!), and pays the rent on her own apartment.

Not surprisingly, we talk every day and see each other often.

She's become her own person, and for better or for worse, she always tells me the truth.

The journey ain't over yet, and Lord only knows what's next in store for us. *It's a long race*, I keep telling myself. *Pace yourself, breathe.*

Maddy still makes me laugh, though, and I'm still trying to quit smoking.

There's no one like her. She is simply amazing.

Maddy's Epilogue

Sobriety has been a tough pill to swallow. Being told the party's over, doctor's orders, at the age of twenty-one, has been an eye-opening experience for me.

I was never obsessed with partying; I just enjoyed it. Having that pleasure yanked away at such a young age just didn't seem fair. My story has never been a story of addiction.

Admitting my drug use taught me to take responsibility for my actions—to hold myself accountable somehow. Pushing the limits wasn't all it was cracked up to be.

Today I'm doing the best I can. The journey doesn't scare me. Like Dorothy figured out when she followed the yellow-brick road, we all have our path.

If I've learned anything from my relationship with my mother, it's that I'm not alone on my path. For better or for worse, she has always been there and will continue to be there.

She's taught me, above everything else, to be myself.

And the fact that she's still speaking to me, after all the things I've put her through, is a testament to her love.

I love her.

And I can't wait to see what happens next.

JOAN'S ACKNOWLEDGMENTS

Thank you, thank you, thank you, to Jen Bergstrom for making all of this happen. You are so smart, so creative, and so incredibly funny. It is truly an honor to have worked with you on something so close to my heart.

To our editor Terra Chalberg, who helped me so much, especially during those moments when I felt like I had definitely bitten off more than I could chew.

Thank you so much to Suzanne Wilson, who read this book more often than I did. Thanks, Suzy, for the unbelievable support and for pretending to be interested when I know for sure you weren't.

Thanks to my sister Kim, for putting up with me obsessing over the writing of the book and repeatedly telling me just to get to work and stop talking about it.

And of course to my son, Ian, for allowing me to tell the odd story about him and trusting me not to embarrass him—at least not too much.

Last but by no means least, thanks to Maddy, for being such an easygoing and fun partner in crime.

Maddy's Acknowledgments

I would first and foremost like to thank Jen Bergstrom, for giving me the opportunity to write this book and helping make it something I can be proud of. I would also like to thank Terra Chalberg, for countless hours of dedicated work. As for my self-appointed "editors," Suzanne Wilson and Sasha Steinberg, thank you for reading it over and over again even though you didn't have to. I would like to thank all of the Simon & Schuster staff, for their support and commitment. I would like to thank my girlies, for endless material and good times—you kept me sane through everything. Last but not least, I would like to thank my family, for stability, loyalty, and love.

Joan Lambur currently lives north of Toronto and splits her time between her career in the children's entertainment business and taking care of Maddy's dog.

Madeleine Lambur is relocating to New York City, where she will continue to write.

Printed in the United States
By Bookmasters